WORKBOOK

THE
POWER
of
TOGETHER

DISCOVER THE CHRISTIAN LIFE
YOU'VE BEEN MISSING

JIM PUTMAN

BakerBooks

a division of Baker Publishing Group
Grand Rapids, Michigan

© 2017 by Jim Putman

Published by Baker Books
a division of Baker Publishing Group
P.O. Box 6287, Grand Rapids, MI 49516-6287
www.bakerbooks.com

Printed in the United States of America

ISBN 978-0-8010-0795-8

17 18 19 20 21 22 23   7 6 5 4 3 2 1

Contents

How to Use This Book

There are people in this world who live on nothing but rice. You can survive on rice alone (barely), but if you want to thrive as a human being, you need to eat a greater variety of foods, including vegetables, fats, and protein. If your diet is missing one of these key ingredients, you won't reach your full physical potential and you'll be vulnerable to certain diseases.

Jesus said, "Man shall not live on bread alone, but on every word that comes from the mouth of God" (Matt. 4:4). He was quoting Moses (Deut. 8:3). Many Christians interpret this statement to mean that they can live on the Word of God, the Bible, alone. As long as they read their Bibles regularly and pray, they can have a personal and fulfilling relationship with God. They have a Jesus-and-me-only kind of relationship.

It's true that you can't have a fulfilling relationship with God without Scripture and prayer, but God intended for us to include another key ingredient in our spiritual food recipe—His Word tells us what else we need to have an abundant life.

Jesus says all the commands in Scripture hang on two commandments, which are intended to lead us to a relationship with God and others:

> "Teacher, which is the greatest commandment in the Law?"
>
> Jesus replied: "'Love the Lord your God with all your heart and with all your soul and with all your mind.' This is the first and greatest commandment. And the second is like it: 'Love your neighbor as yourself.' All the Law and the Prophets hang on these two commandments." (Matt. 22:36–40)

Why does God tell us through His Word that we must be in relationships? Well, because God made us relational beings and He knows we need relationships to thrive. In other words, spiritual relationships as God designs and empowers them are a vital part of the recipe for abundant life.

Think of it: we were created for perfect relationship with God and others, but we lost this ability because of sin. God has been seeking to restore us to His perfect design. He gives us a recipe for spiritual food that will help us live, but we must decide to follow the Expert Chef's directions if we are to be all He created us to be.

This workbook is designed to help you learn to love well. It will teach you about relationships, and if you go through it with a group, you will learn through relationships by practicing them. The goal of this workbook is transformation, not merely information. Ideally, you'll work through the text and questions for about twenty minutes a day, five days a week, and then meet with a group for about ninety minutes each week to discuss your answers and support each other through sharing and prayer. Be sure to read the Growing Together section at the end of each Day 5 to prepare for your group session.

Notice that any boldface Scripture references or "passages" in the text direct you to the accompanying Scripture found in the margins.

Do take the time to answer the questions on your own. Many of them deal with your own personal responses to what the text is teaching. Be as honest as you can be. If you've never experienced the scenario or practiced the principle being discussed, it's okay to say so. If you have experienced it, it's okay to be completely candid about what happened when you write your answers. Then when you meet with your group, you can share as much as you can without gossiping. You might want to leave out the names of the people involved, for example, and be careful when discussing details that could identify them.

The ideal group size is three to ten people. If your group is larger than ten, consider dividing in two for the discussion. When you share prayer requests, consider doing so in subgroups of five or six people.

If you are leading the group discussion, you will find suggestions for structuring your meeting at the end of this guide.

If you are in a group, remember that what is said in the group stays in the group. It must be a safe place for all involved, and gossip is sin. Remember also that your goal is not to fix each other—allow people to be honest and only help if you are invited to. Finally, remember to not dominate the conversation; the goal is for everyone to be able to share. If you are shy, please be courageous and share at least a little. Hopefully over time you will start to trust those around you and will experience the support God has always wanted you to have. Our hope is that you will join in building a safe group where you can be honest and experience all that God intended for Christian relationships.

Week 1

Go and Make Grown-ups

Do you feel in over your head when facing some of the expectations of vibrant Christian living, let alone the demands of life in general? Do you read in the Scriptures, for example, that the fruit of God's Holy Spirit in our lives is love, joy, peace, patience, and so forth (Gal. 5:22), but these qualities are not overflowing in your life? Do you read about Jesus sending His followers into the world for ministry, and you assume that applies to the professional clergy only, because there's no way you have the skill and space in your life to be drawing outsiders into the fold of God's people?

There might be a significant reason for your feelings. Maybe you were born anew into God's family some time ago, but then nobody parented you spiritually so you would grow into a mature, responsible, and equipped believer. Maybe you were just handed a Bible and heard some weekly sermons, and it was implied that those were all you needed to grow up.

But that's not all you need. Just as babies need parent figures to actively, intentionally prepare them throughout childhood for adult maturity and responsibility, so also God has placed us in a spiritual family for parallel purposes. In both our physical and spiritual families, God intends family members to engage in open, two-way, give-and-take relationships. These healthy relationships are not only integral to the maturing process but critical to fulfill our designed needs as well as our God-given goals.

When this relational dynamic is somehow cut short or done wrongly, we enter into life as supposedly mature followers of Jesus, but we are unprepared and often overwhelmed. Someone didn't do his or her job. Or maybe they tried, but we short-circuited God's plan by refusing to become part of the family of God. We wanted salvation but not a new life.

In three of my previous books, I have taught that we are called to be and make disciples, and we do this in a relational environment. Unfortunately, the typical church is something you attend once a week and has no plan to intentionally disciple in relationship. There are few spiritual parents who will walk believers through to spiritual maturity, where you can become all you were designed to be.

Previously I have taught that in relationship we progress through defined stages of spiritual growth. I have taught that every Christian is a disciple meant to grow to spiritual maturity—parenthood—and that all are saved and gifted to make disciples. As you read *The Power of Together* and complete this companion workbook, I'll endeavor to help you understand anything from those foundations that you need as you, an individual Christian in probably a typical Christian church, seek to practice relational discipleship in your circles and support its implementation in your life and church.

The process starts by challenging today's popular Christian definition of *maturity*. Many in the Christian world define maturity for a Jesus-follower primarily in terms of *what you know* or *what you can do*, or both. And those are both indispensable components of maturity in Christ. But they're not the whole package.

Many who think they're practicing relational discipleship are still missing the real, biblical point. They use relationships—profitably—to convey information and to coach and model behaviors. Again, that's excellent for those limited purposes. But if relationships aren't used *to help people become relational* (loving God and loving others), then we have still missed out on true maturity.

The one thing I hope you take away from this experience is that, by the Bible's own definition, *a mature disciple is a great lover of God and a great lover of people* (see Jesus's greatest commands, Matt. 22:37–40). Yes, disciples *know* stuff, but they seek to learn because they *love*, and out of love, they learn. Yes, disciples *do* stuff, but they serve with their gifts because they love, and in serving they discover loving relationships that help them thrive and that are attractive to a world starving for real relationship. (We'll learn more about how this works in Weeks 1 through 6.)

I hope this study also helps you more fully learn and live a second biblical reality: *Loving relationships, with God and with people, form the context in which all effective discipleship takes place.* In Matthew 28:18–20, Jesus charged His church to "make disciples" both by "baptizing them" and by "teaching them to obey everything I have commanded you." Remember that He had discipled them for three years, so when He commanded them to make disciples, He was telling them to do what He had done for them. Jesus made disciples in relationship. True teaching, as Jesus defined it, had to be done in relationship. He wasn't saying, "Go disciple any way you want to." He was saying, "Go do what I did."

In Weeks 7 through 9 we'll delve into a few aspects of the human experience—a few critical skills for living—that traditional discipleship sometimes overlooks.

Now, because there's so much confusion about what a disciple is, we'll spend the rest of this week exploring some of the concepts that serve as a foundation for the rest of the study.

Day 1: Disciples, Not Converts

The New Testament metaphor of baptism is a picture of new birth (being born again) into the Christian family, the church. In Christ we are now adopted into the household of God, and even more, we are born into a family with older brothers and sisters. Paul called himself Timothy's father in the faith and so it is supposed to be with us—we have spiritual parents.

If we have physical parents who know and love Jesus, then it is the Lord's intention that they be the primary disciple-makers in our lives. When this happens, Christian families become a source of spiritual parenthood for others who were not similarly blessed with mature Christ-following parents. These people need the church—God's family that helps others find Christ and then become mature in Him. Even if we have been blessed with believing, mature, disciple-making parents, they were never intended to be the only ones who help us mature—again, the church is God's plan for growing mature disciples who make disciples. Pastors and teachers will also speak into our lives. We will have other believers for the rest of our lives who will teach and encourage us. God's plan is that we will grow to maturity and invest in others as well.

Maturity does not mean that we have no more to learn, or that somehow we are complete and have no need of continual relationships and growth in our lives—that never ends. But Christians are by nature family to one another—we'll say a lot about that in this workbook. However, there comes a time when we are able to invest in others. Even if we are only one step ahead of a person, we can still lead them as we progress.

As in any family, the parents and other mature family members are the ones who are supposed to do the primary work to raise the newborn to maturity. Think about the rare instances when a child somehow survives absolute physical abandonment. What is the

Jesus . . . said, "All authority in heaven and on earth has been given to me. Therefore go and make disciples of all nations, baptizing them in the name of the Father and of the Son and of the Holy Spirit, and teaching them to obey everything I have commanded you. And surely I am with you always, to the very end of the age."
(Matt. 28:18–20)

result? An infant in adult form. The twenty-year-old "adult" has few social skills, poor language, few of the benefits of teaching and modeling by others. He or she knows little about healthy living—physically, relationally, spiritually. This adult, never having met anyone of the opposite sex, doesn't even know where a new child comes from.

That's why Jesus's Great Commission included two subcommands: "baptizing them . . . and teaching them to obey" (see **Matt. 28:18–20**). Jesus knew we would forget the innate necessity of the second, so He made it a command. And yet we neglect it, allowing our spiritual offspring to raise themselves or be raised by the world. Few survive spiritually, and those who do end up as spiritual brats who don't look like Christ. Brats who take on the name of Jesus end up misrepresenting Jesus to the world. No wonder so few of the spiritually dead—those who have not accepted Christ—want to join the dysfunctional family we call the church. No wonder so many are leaving after spending time in our broken version of God's family.

Part of the problem might be that when someone shared their faith with us, they didn't tell us or show us there was something next. If they did tell us anything, it came in the form of a tract or a Bible handed to us with the instruction "Come to church next week." It's almost as though we were told we had finished the race rather than started one. Sadly, many of us accepted Christ based on emotion as the song "Just As I Am" was sung seventeen times until we walked down the aisle. Someone prayed with us but didn't explain anything after that. It was as if the infant's job was to figure it out for himself after that. The person now had hell insurance but no directions for life that came with help in any form.

When Jesus sent out His disciples to make disciples, He didn't just say, "Go do it any way you want to." He spent a couple of years showing them what it looked like. He was saying, "You saw Me; now go and repeat." And they did.

Many people study the commands of Jesus and the teachings of Jesus but don't really look at the context in which He gave them.

Jesus had a process that He took His guys through that we can look at. We call it the SCMD process:

- *Share:* Jesus *shared* who He was.
- *Connect:* Those who responded He invited into *connection* (relationship) with Him. As they spent time with Jesus, He would say, "You have heard . . . but I tell you . . ." He taught them spiritual truth, and they learned to be in relationship with God the Father as they followed Jesus, the exact representation of His being. They learned what it meant to obey God as they watched Jesus do it. They learned how to love one another as Jesus challenged their foolish self-centeredness.
- *Minister:* In connection, He began to train them for *ministry.* They watched Him heal, confront, teach. He sent them out by twos and then debriefed. He was making ministers out of them.
- *Disciple:* Finally, He sent them out to do what He had done: to make *disciples.*

The early church did the same thing:

- The apostles *shared* who Jesus was.
- Those who responded *connected* with each other in the temple courts and from house to house. Those who became Christians devoted themselves to the apostles' teaching, so they learned to replace what they had been handed with a whole new way of seeing life and love.
- From the apostles and one another, the believers learned to become *ministers,* serving others. They sold their possessions to take care of the needy. Seven of them became deacons and ministered to the Greek-speaking widows.
- Philip became a *disciple-maker* in Samaria.

Jesus	The Early Church
Share: Luke 5:1–4; Matthew 4:19	**Share:** Acts 2:1–39
Connect: Mark 9:30; John 3:22	**Connect:** Acts 2:40–Acts 4:37
Minister: Luke 9:1–7	**Minister:** Acts 6
Disciple: Matthew 28	**Disciple:** Acts 8

If we desire the results of Jesus, we must be careful not to divorce the teachings of Jesus from the methods of Jesus.

1. When you became a follower of Jesus, were you told what came next and what to expect? Were you invited into a relationship (connection) with a more mature Christian, or were you left to try to figure out the Christian life on your own? Describe your early experience.

----

2. How has your early experience of having or not having someone to disciple you affected your spiritual growth?

----

3. Have you been taught that you are called to become a minister and a disciple-maker? Or have you assumed that those are pastors' jobs? Describe what you've been taught or what you assumed about your responsibility as a follower of Jesus.

----

4. How has that affected what you do or what you don't do in the church?

----

5. How do you respond to the idea that you are called to minister and make disciples?

_____

_____

_____

_____

6. How could you benefit from being connected relationally with other followers of Christ—spiritual parents and siblings? Or if you don't think you could benefit, why not?

_____

_____

_____

_____

Day 2: What Is a Disciple?

Jesus was intentional, and He had an end goal in mind when He began His earthly ministry. First, obviously He came to die for our sins, but second, He came to make disciples who could take that message to a lost world. What good is it if we have the greatest news in history, but we aren't sharing it and living it out?

We strive to have everyone in our church know that our intention is to make disciples of Jesus. Many churches state their purpose is to "make disciples," but much of their effort, resources, and time go toward building up attendance or caring for the facilities. If we don't know what Jesus meant by "go and make disciples," we will not know when we have fulfilled His command. We must define what a disciple of Jesus is if we are to have success.

While walking by the Sea of Galilee, he saw two brothers, Simon (who is called Peter) and Andrew his brother, casting a net into the sea, for they were fishermen. And he said to them, "Follow me, and I will make you fishers of men." Immediately they left their nets and followed him. (Matt. 4:18–20 ESV)

In **Matthew 4:18–20**, we find the definition of discipleship in Jesus's commands when He told His disciples right from the beginning what He intended:

- *"Follow me."* I am the Master. I lead and you follow.
- *"I will make you . . ."* Into one who looks like the Master, a lover of God and others.
- *"Fishers of men."* Those who will fulfill His mission.

In other words,

- *A disciple is a follower of Christ.* Disciples know who Jesus is and have decided to follow Him as Lord and King, because they understand the truth about their lostness and are grateful for what God in Christ was willing to do for them.
- *A disciple is being changed by Christ* (into one who looks like Him) through His Word, His Spirit, and His people.

- *A disciple is committed to the mission of Christ*—that is, to ensure the repeated, perpetual completion of the first two. The mature disciple uses his or her skills, gifts, experiences, and resources to further the mission of Jesus—to seek and to save the lost and make disciples who make disciples.

This book focuses primarily on the middle component of our definition of a disciple revealed in Matthew 4:19—being changed by Christ. When we say we are being changed by Christ, we mean that we are becoming like Christ or being conformed into His image as we journey with Him (**Rom. 8:29**). There is so much packed into that statement, but when we boil it down, Jesus says all the law and the prophets are summed up in loving the Lord your God and loving your neighbor as yourself. Jesus is the living Word and the perfect living picture of the fulfillment of the law—He was able to die in our stead because He fulfilled every aspect perfectly. If all the law hangs on love for God and others, then Jesus is the perfect model to follow, and with the Holy Spirit's help in a variety of ways, we are being shaped to look more and more like Him.

For those God foreknew he also predestined to be conformed to the image of his Son, that he might be the firstborn among many brothers and sisters. (Rom. 8:29)

My reason for focusing on this aspect of spiritual maturity is because it is often the least implemented principle in the discipleship definition. Many people focus on the knowledge of and obedience to Jesus as essential to biblical maturity, and rightly so. Many others focus on skills and gifts used by believers as essential to maturity, and again rightly so, as this is also part of the whole picture. However, many neglect a key facet: being in relationship as a defining characteristic of Christ-followers (John 13:35). Discipleship is a process in which relationship is both the goal and the context for reaching that goal.

Let's break this down. First, notice that Jesus makes it clear that a disciple is one who follows Jesus. Disciples follow because they know who He is: God the Son, part of the Trinity. They have accepted the testimony of the Old Testament Scriptures about the coming Messiah. Jesus was born to a virgin in Bethlehem, all according to Scripture. Jesus proved who He was with His sinless life and the miraculous signs He performed. God testified who

Jesus was when He said from heaven, "This is my Son, whom I love; with him I am well pleased" (Matt. 3:17). Jesus went to the cross just as Isaiah said He would, and He rose from the dead to declare He had paid the price for the sin of all who would accept Him as Lord and Savior. A disciple is one who has accepted Jesus for who He truly is: Lord, King, and loving Savior to all who would follow.

Jesus gave the invitation to come and follow. Notice He does not force us; He invites us to come, and we, as disciples, say yes and follow. So to make this clear, we are disciples of Jesus only if we believe He is who He says He is and we choose to follow Him. We are not a disciple of Jesus if we are not growing in our trust and obedience of Jesus.

Second, as disciples of Jesus, we have received the Holy Spirit, who is changing us from the inside out. As Romans 8:29 tells us, we are being conformed into the likeness of Jesus—we are becoming more and more like Him as we grow in our faith and spend time following Him. If we are not becoming like Jesus, then we are either not a disciple of Jesus or very new in the process. What are the defining characteristics of Jesus that are rubbing off on you? Jesus is the perfect example of one who loves God and others, so to be changed by Christ means that you are taking on His values, priorities, and characteristics. The fruit (behaviors and attitudes) that reveals you are a follower of Jesus is the fruit of the Spirit (**Gal. 5:22–23**). All of the fruit of the Spirit is relational in nature. The fruit of the Spirit is love for whom? Peace with whom? Patience with whom? And so on. These characteristics are found in Christ as the ultimate example of what it looks like in a physical being to love God and others.

Third, a disciple of Jesus is becoming more and more committed to the mission of Christ. We believe what Jesus says about eternity, we know Jesus has loved us and saved us, and we know that Jesus loves a lost world. Therefore, we love Him and those He loves so much that we seek to share the gospel with a lost world. If you claim to be a disciple of Jesus but are not interested in fishing for people, then there is something wrong with your

But the fruit of the Spirit is love, joy, peace, forbearance, kindness, goodness, faithfulness, gentleness and self-control. Against such things there is no law. (Gal. 5:22–23)

understanding of the faith. Paul tells us with tears in his eyes that many are enemies of the cross of Christ, and he set his goal to preach to a lost world. This is an essential part of spiritual maturity.

Thus, as we proceed through Jesus's process of sharing, connecting, training for ministry, and being released to make disciples, we are learning to follow Jesus more and more, we are becoming like Jesus (lovers of God and others) more and more, and we are becoming committed to the mission of Jesus with all the resources that have been deposited in us more and more.

1. Where are you in the process described above? Are you learning to follow Jesus? Are you learning to be like Jesus in His love for the Father and for others? Are you becoming committed to Jesus's mission of making disciples?

2. Think about whether and how you are growing in your obedience to Christ. Using Galatians 5:22–23 above as a self-assessment tool, in which areas has the Holy Spirit made considerable progress in producing His fruit in you? In which areas does He need to do more work?

3. Is there an area in your life that you need to share with your group (or one trusted person), confessing your sin and asking for accountability? What are you struggling with?

4. Forgiving others is one measure of your love for God and others. Is there someone you need to forgive? (This doesn't mean saying that what they did to you is okay; it simply means dropping your inner demand that they pay for what they did.) Do you need to ask for someone else's forgiveness? If so, whose?

_____

_____

_____

_____

5. Who are you praying for to receive Jesus as Savior and King?

_____

_____

_____

_____

Day 3: Every Disciple Becomes Complete by Becoming a Disciple-Maker

The scientific definition of life includes reproduction: life includes any organism that is able to reproduce itself. A virus is not alive; it needs to use an infected host's cells for reproduction.

Something without life cannot reproduce—it has no "choice." However, a living organism, designed to reproduce, may or may not actually make more of itself. For many practical purposes—especially species survival, the avoidance of extinction—a life that doesn't reproduce is a failure, falling short of one of its main purposes. In some ways, it is as good as dead.

If you have been called by Christ to be His disciple, then you have built into your spiritual DNA both the ability and the calling to become a disciple-maker. When you were born again, you were made able to grow into a reproducing spiritual parent. You don't finish the race at conversion, just as a baby isn't finished at birth. You are part of something greater. We are all called to maturity, and by definition that means all of us—not just the paid professionals—help others become mature.

The writer of **Hebrews** makes it clear in **5:11–14** that all disciples were called to teach others in the faith.

Jesus had made it clear to His disciples that they were going to become fishers of men (Matt. 4:19), and at the end of their discipleship journey with Jesus, they were sent to do what they had been trained to do—go and make disciples. Many people today like to make the distinction between a Christian and a disciple, but the Scriptures do not give us this out. The early church called itself the disciples in the beginning, and the role of a disciple is to make disciples. We do this as individuals wherever we live, work, and play. We also do this as a corporate body—the church—as each of us uses the spiritual gifts and abilities that were knit into us in our mothers' wombs. We use our resources financially to help support the mission of the church.

We have much to say about this, but it is hard to make it clear to you because you no longer try to understand. In fact, though by this time you ought to be teachers, you need someone to teach you the elementary truths of God's word all over again. You need milk, not solid food! Anyone who lives on milk, being still an infant, is not acquainted with the teaching about righteousness. But solid food is for the mature, who by constant use have trained themselves to distinguish good from evil. (Heb. 5:11–14)

23

For we are God's masterpiece. He has created us anew in Christ Jesus, so we can do the good things he planned for us long ago. (Eph. 2:10 NLT)

He is the one we proclaim, admonishing and teaching everyone with all wisdom, so that we may present everyone fully mature in Christ. (Col. 1:28)

And the things you have heard me say in the presence of many witnesses entrust to reliable people who will also be qualified to teach others. (2 Tim. 2:2)

You see, God had a purpose for each of us before time began (**Eph. 2:10**). The process of growing up spiritually is the process of discovering the purpose that God has for each of us within the context of the world we live in and the church we are part of.

As we are discipled, we are growing to maturity in Christ (**Col. 1:28**). This happens with the help of mature spiritual disciple-makers (parents) within the context of the church, as we see Paul did with Timothy (**2 Tim. 2:2**). One part of a parent's job is to help children discover how they were designed by God and then help them discover possible places they can use their gifts.

1. How do you respond to the idea that a Christian life that doesn't reproduce is falling short of one of its main purposes? Have you been intentional about passing your faith to others? If not, what could you do to begin?

   _____

   _____

   _____

2. What help would you need from your Christian family (spiritual parents and siblings) in order for you to reproduce by leading someone else to Christ? Be sure to share this with your group.

   _____

   _____

   _____

3. What help do you need to discover your place in the church family, where you can serve and others can benefit from how God designed you?

   _____

   _____

   _____

The Scriptures not only reveal the end goal of every believer (maturity), they also reveal a process of maturing. They show us stages of spiritual growth. We all start out as dead, and then discipleship is the process of coming alive and then growing up spiritually.

Every person starts out dead because of sin (Rom. 3:23). When they were born again, they became an infant in Christ. As they grow, they become children, then later young adults, and finally mature spiritual parents who help others find new birth and maturity. Because God's plan is to use people (the family of God, the church) to help others grow up, we use descriptions for each stage so that we can teach every believer to identify our own place and others' places in the process of spiritual growth. The descriptions help us realize when we are being immature so that we can change our own behavior, but they also help us know where others are so we can help them grow. The goal of identifying where we or others are is not to judge but to help us all take the next step in the spiritual journey. The end goal is to intentionally help people develop into spiritual parents (disciple-makers) so they can help birth people into Christ and grow them to maturity. In our church we teach everyone that they are saved for the purpose of helping the dead come to life in Christ, and if God uses you to help birth them, then He also wants you to help raise them.

These are the five stages and some of the characteristics of people in each stage:

Dead. Characterized by ignorance, unbelief, and rebellion. They might say, "I don't know which God is God"; "There is no God"; "There are many ways to heaven"; "There is no hell"; "I don't need to be saved because I am a good person." Jesus is not Lord to them, and they will not follow or surrender.

Infants. Characterized by ignorance and even excitement. They believe Jesus is the Son of God who has saved them from hell. They can be thankful and even inspiring as the Lord brings them out of the dead world. They can add so much to a group because they remind you of when you were brand new and excited. They are often curious and may want to share Jesus with all their friends who see a change. But they don't know much of what Scripture says. They don't know

Dead: *As for you, you were dead in your transgressions and sins, in which you used to live when you followed the ways of this world and of the ruler of the kingdom of the air, the spirit who is now at work in those who are disobedient. All of us also lived among them at one time, gratifying the cravings of our flesh and following its desires and thoughts. Like the rest, we were by nature deserving of wrath. (Eph. 2:1–3)*

Infants: *Like newborn babies, crave pure spiritual milk, so that by*

it you may grow up in your salvation. (1 Pet. 2:2)

Infants and the mature: *Anyone who lives on milk, being still an infant, is not acquainted with the teaching about righteousness. But solid food is for the mature, who by constant use have trained themselves to distinguish good from evil. (Heb. 5:13–14)*

Children/young adults/parents:
I am writing to you, dear children,
   because your sins have been for-
      given on account of his name.
I am writing to you, fathers,
   because you know him who is from
      the beginning.
I am writing to you, young men,
   because you have overcome the
      evil one.

I write to you, dear children,
   because you know the Father.
I write to you, fathers,
   because you know him who is from
      the beginning.
I write to you, young men,
   because you are strong,
   and the word of God lives in you,
   and you have overcome the evil
      one. (1 John 2:12–14)

how Jesus and His followers modeled the life of faith. They tend to be consumers and need protection and pouring into. They can be easy targets for the enemy, who loves to prey on the young the way lions target a newborn who strays too far from its mother.

Children. Characterized by lingering self-centeredness. They know Christian language and so can spiritualize their comments, but they are me-centered. They might say, "I don't like that church because I don't like the music"; "I didn't get anything out of that sermon"; "The pastor didn't notice me"; "I had to walk two blocks to get to home group/church." They are often rigid and unwilling to give much grace, but they expect a lot of it. They tend to do the right thing as long as it produces the outcome they desire. They are often not yet willing to obey Jesus when it is costly, as they still see Jesus as the one who ought to make their lives what they want them to be rather than what He desires them to be. They tend to have a consumer mind-set and will notice problems but often are unwilling to be a part of the solution. They tend to crave the honeymoon experience—they want to experience things that make them feel good and don't like to be uncomfortable. They, like infants, can bring great joy to your life, just as a child does in the home, but they are a lot of work too.

Young adults. Characterized by zeal and independence. They are committed and think they have the answers, much like adolescents in the physical world. They want to serve independently, and they have come to understand that they really can do many things parents can do. They make great spiritual babysitters but are not intentional and so are not good parents. They can be idealistic, tending to see things simply in black and white. They have the capacity to be others-centered. They truly love God and others and will jump into complex situations only to discover that they are in over their heads. They are players but have not made the transition to coaches yet. In other words, they need and want to contribute, but they require guidance, as they are not wise yet. They are naive about the dangers of pride and discouragement, so they need a spiritual parent or guide to process ministry with them, or the devil can play havoc in their lives.

Spiritual parents. Characterized by wanting God's will more than their own. They are others-centered and intentional about raising people up to their spiritual potential. While not perfect, they are consistently humble, honest, transparent, encouraging, and courageous. They fight for solid relationships by dealing with conflict when it arises. They are faithful and committed to the Lord and others no matter what. They forgive and ask for forgiveness when and if they make mistakes. They are purposely pouring into others and see them as future disciple-makers with gifts. Their spiritual children are looking more and more like Jesus. Success is getting others in the game and coaching them. They are contributors as they see needs and step into those holes for the body of Christ. They are people who lead as Jesus led—humbly and as a servant. They are also people under submission—servants who follow the God-given authority in their lives.

4. Think of some Christians you know. How would you go about identifying each of them as an infant, a child, a young adult, or a parent? Which of them would you go to for help or counsel?

Jesus tells us that out of the overflow of the heart the mouth speaks (Matt. 12:34), so relationship and time spent in conversation will often reveal a person's level of maturity. Likewise, Jesus tells us in Matthew 7:16 that we can know a tree by its fruit (consistent behavior), so watching what people do also tells us their stage of maturity.

We don't learn these stages in order to sit back and judge others but so that we can encourage others to be who they have been saved to become. (We all have brat moments and need encouragement or admonition.) We can also recognize our own stage of maturity by thinking about the words we use and the way we act.

Here is how we put the SCMD process together with the spiritual stages: We *share* our lives with the dead, and when they become open, we share the gospel with them. Once a spiritual baby is born, we continue to share our lives with the infant. Don't think an infant has the ability to pursue you—you must pursue them just as a mother must care for her baby and not put it on the couch and say, "There is the fridge, there is the toilet."

As the infant grows into a child, we help them *connect* with the rest of the family (brothers and sisters). In this connection environment, we train children to connect to God in a personal relationship. We help them discover what this means. We also help them see how they can connect to the mission God has saved them for.

As they continue to mature, we begin to help them *minister* with supervision. At the minister stage of the process, they are learning to serve without expectation. They are becoming contributors and see others as more important than themselves. Every child learns to serve in a family, using their God-given gifts and abilities. As children grow into young adults, we allow them to serve with much less supervision.

Finally, when a young adult is responsible and committed enough to care for others intentionally, we release these spiritual parents to make *disciples* on their own.

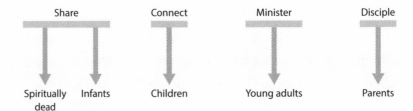

5. What elements in the descriptions of the stages are helpful to you?

6. Based on these descriptions, where are you in the process of growth: dead, infant, child, young adult, or parent? Be specific about the things that fit you right now in describing your stage.

7. At the stage where you are, what do you need from God and your spiritual family to continue to mature?

Day 4: Jesus, the Greatest Disciple-Maker

They came to Capernaum. When he was in the house, he asked them, "What were you arguing about on the road?" But they kept quiet because on the way they had argued about who was the greatest.

Sitting down, Jesus called the Twelve and said, "Anyone who wants to be first must be the very last, and the servant of all."

He took a little child whom he placed among them. Taking the child in his arms, he said to them, "Whoever welcomes one of these little children in my name welcomes me; and whoever welcomes me does not welcome me but the one who sent me." (Mark 9:33–37)

[The first few thousand of Jesus's followers] devoted themselves to the apostles' teaching and to the fellowship, to the breaking of bread and to prayer. . . . All the believers were together and had everything in common. They sold property and possessions to give to anyone who had need. Every day they continued to meet together in the temple courts. They broke bread in their homes and ate together with glad and sincere hearts, praising God and enjoying the favor of all the people.

When Jesus told His disciple-makers to go and make disciples, He did not mean, "Go do it any way you want." We follow His lead in how to do this. We must marry the teachings of Jesus with the methods of Jesus in order to get the results of Jesus.

How did Jesus get His results?

Many teachers today may preach a sermon about the importance of humility or how special children are, but Jesus taught differently. Notice that Jesus taught by hanging out and by modeling. Jesus responded to a behavior He noticed in His disciples as they were doing life together. He did something they would never forget. He gave them a visual that burned its way into their memory. These methods are accomplished in a relational context. See **Mark 9:33–37**. The early church followed His example. See **Acts 2:42, 44–47**.

Observe these New Testament spiritual generations:

- Barnabas invested in Paul via relationship.
- Paul did the same in Timothy, Luke, Silas, Mark, and many more.
- And Paul told Timothy to invest in reliable people, who would reproduce themselves in others (**2 Tim. 2:2**).

We recognize that a Christian is to be characterized by love for God and others, and yet so often we teach this in such a way that people cannot see it lived out and therefore have difficulty implementing it in their lives. Near the end of Jesus's earthly ministry, He was walking with His disciples and they were arguing. After all this time with Jesus, they were still fighting over who was the greatest in the kingdom of heaven. They were stuck in pride. Have you ever thought about what He must have been thinking as He heard them? Imagine Him thinking, *You know what—I need to preach a three-part sermon series on humility.* No. Not that He didn't preach about humility. He had done so. But now, Jesus did something more. When He got to the house where they would eat the Last Supper, He took off most of His clothes, wrapped a towel around His waist, and washed their feet. He then told them that the Son of Man had not come to be served but to serve. Jesus didn't preach a sermon as we normally would think of it. He preached through modeling, in relationship.

Most people think a person is mature because they have been to church and sat through the sermons and classes—maybe they even went to Bible college and passed the written exams. However, when that is the only test, we can't really know if someone is mature, because we haven't been with them to see what they really act like in their everyday life. We haven't seen their level of maturity displayed in real-life situations.

In relationship we get to know who a person really is—not the rote answers they spooled out in the test but the real ones evidenced in times of testings. Jesus made disciples in relationship, and His disciples watched Him deal with the first year of popularity, the second year of suspicion, and the third year of persecution. He did this because it's only in relationship that you really come to know people. It's only in relationship that you can really show people what it looks like to live a humble life. Modeling, practice, accountability, and discussion can only happen when you really have relationship.

Another reason for relationship is that most people are not called to teaching and preaching in the sense that Ephesians 4:11 discusses. Most have different gifts—such as mercy and encouragement and hospitality—that are to be used within the context of relationships. Most won't preach sermons like evangelists, with crowds listening and responding. But everyone is called to be and make disciples, so it makes sense that we must help people learn to do this within the context of the lives they lead every day. Not everyone can preach, but everyone can wash someone's feet (metaphorically) and talk to them. Everyone can see a need and meet it and then talk to the person who wonders why they loved them in this way.

And the Lord added to their number daily those who were being saved. (Acts 2:42, 44–47)

And the things you have heard me say in the presence of many witnesses entrust to reliable people who will also be qualified to teach others. (2 Tim. 2:2)

Relationship is the best context to make disciples, whether at church, at work, or at home with your children. And your relationship with God and His family is what enables you to become more like the Lord Jesus. Relationship (along with biblical understanding) makes you mature.

1. Why is relationship the best context for spiritual growth?

   _____

   _____

   _____

2. On a scale of 1 to 5, how good are you currently at relationships that promote spiritual growth in yourself and in others? Explain why you chose the number you did.

1	2	3	4	5
Lousy at growth-fostering relationships				Great at growth-fostering relationships

   _____

   _____

   _____

3. Which of your relationships have the most potential for fostering growth in yourself and others? Which ones are currently fostering growth? What is it about those relationships that is fostering this growth?

   _____

   _____

   _____

4. In Mark 9:33–37, why do you think Jesus involved a child in His discussion with His disciples? Why didn't He just explain His thoughts on humility? What is it about *being* an example rather than *teaching* a lesson that works more effectively?

   _____

   _____

   _____

5. Why did Jesus wash His disciples' feet? Why not just give them the instruction to love and serve each other?

Day 5: Something Is Missing

I felt compelled to write and urge you to contend for the faith that was once for all entrusted to God's holy people. . . .

But you, dear friends, by building yourselves up in your most holy faith and praying in the Holy Spirit, keep yourselves in God's love as you wait for the mercy of our Lord Jesus Christ to bring you to eternal life.

Be merciful to those who doubt; save others by snatching them from the fire; to others show mercy, mixed with fear—hating even the clothing stained by corrupted flesh. (Jude 3, 20–23)

Why do so few people today experience the abundant Christian life?

"The faith that was once for all entrusted" (**Jude 3**) doesn't, in this context, mean the gospel alone, but also how we live out the life of faith, as Jude admonishes (**vv. 20–23**). What are the components that Jesus has included in "the faith"—the spiritual recipe for the abundant life He promises? And what happens when we forget an important ingredient from Jesus's recipe?

When we actively omit or passively neglect some ingredient—discipling people by some incomplete "recipe" toward some incomplete definition of maturity—they experience less than God's intended best. So many Christians rebelliously or ignorantly create a recipe of the faith that they are comfortable with but then are frustrated by the results. I want to make this clear—God has no obligation to bless or work in *your* version of the faith. He blesses and works within His version as we obey His directions. Sadly, many are living out the version they were handed, and then when it doesn't fulfill them, they leave the church with a false understanding of the faith, thinking Jesus is not real.

We must abide or remain in Jesus, and He says this happens when we obey Him (John 15:10). In other words, we surrender to His commands concerning faith, love, and relationship.

Because relationships have been broken by sin, that which was supposed to be a blessing has become a curse in many ways. Therefore, to protect ourselves, too often we decide to have no relationships or only shallow ones. However, when we accept the comfortable and safe as we see it, rather than obeying Jesus, we are acting contrary to the faith once for all delivered to the saints.

We live in a world at war, and the devil (our enemy) is trying to deceive us and kill us, so we must decide to do what Jesus has asked us to do. When we are told to contend for the faith entrusted, He is telling us to live out all that was handed down to us in every aspect of the faith as described in God's Word. He is not just talking about the doctrinal truths—like the Trinity, and justification and sanctification—but the whole of the faith modeled by Jesus and lived out by the disciples.

Ever since Adam and Eve's failure in the garden, the devil has taken God's words and ever so slightly cast doubt on them to deceive us. "Did God *really* say . . . ?" "Is the Bible *really* inspired or does it just contain God's words in fallible human form?" "His commands are really just good suggestions." "A loving God wouldn't really condemn anyone to hell."

Just as rat poison is about 99 percent safe but uses the other 1 percent to kill, so the devil uses Scripture but redefines or twists a word to strip it of its truth and power.

1. What is one aspect of the faith entrusted to you that isn't simply doctrine? For example, when Jesus washes His disciples' feet in **John 13**, is He giving us a new command to obey or showing us an example of humility?

   _____
   _____
   _____

2. Have you experienced pain or frustration in relationships that made you leery of deep relationships with other Christians? If so, describe your experience and how it has affected you.

   _____
   _____
   _____

3. How can we pursue growth-fostering relationships with other Christians that take into account the fact that all people are flawed?

   _____
   _____
   _____

Jesus knew that the Father had put all things under his power, and that he had come from God and was returning to God; so he got up from the meal, took off his outer clothing, and wrapped a towel around his waist. After that, he poured water into a basin and began to wash his disciples' feet, drying them with the towel that was wrapped around him.

He came to Simon Peter, who said to him, "Lord, are you going to wash my feet?"

Jesus replied, "You do not realize now what I am doing, but later you will understand."

"No," said Peter, "you shall never wash my feet."

Jesus answered, "Unless I wash you, you have no part with me."

"Then, Lord," Simon Peter replied, "not just my feet but my hands and my head as well!"

Jesus answered, "Those who have had a bath need only to wash their feet; their whole body is clean. And you are clean, though not every one of you." For he knew who was going to betray him, and that was why he said not every one was clean.

When he had finished washing their feet, he put on his clothes and returned to his place. "Do you understand what I have done for you?" he asked them. "You call me 'Teacher' and 'Lord,' and rightly so, for that is what I am. Now that I, your Lord and Teacher, have washed your feet, you also should wash one another's feet. I have set you an example that you should do as I have done for you. Very truly I tell you, no servant is greater than his master, nor is a messenger greater than the one who sent him. Now that you know these things, you will be blessed if you do them. (John 13:3–17)

4. What are the key insights you have had in Week 1 of this study? What do you want to take from this week and apply to your life?

_____

_____

_____

Growing Together

This section provides recommended weekly group discussion material drawn from the daily lessons.

At some point during this initial meeting, discuss how to make your group a safe place for people to share their pain and struggles. Agree that whatever is shared in the group is confidential and stays within the group. Also, practice listening to each other with care and without trying to fix one another.

Day 1: Review questions 1 and 3. Consider sharing one of those responses with your small group. Looking at question 6, discuss with the group what you believe you need from spiritual parents and siblings.

Day 2: Review question 3, and for those who feel comfortable, share an area in which you would like accountability. (For support, revisit this in later meetings.)

Collect the names from question 5 to make a prayer list. If you don't want to share a name, identify the person as, for example, "my son's piano teacher." (Pray for them at the end of each group session.)

Day 3: Review your responses to questions 2, 3, and 7 and share them with your group.

Day 4: Talk about how your group can be a place for relationships that foster growth for each person to move toward the next step of spiritual maturity.

Day 5: Discuss the key insights you have had in Week 1.

Take a few moments to pray for the names on Day 2's prayer list.

Week 2

The Gospel of Relationship

In 2003 the Commission on Children at Risk published a study called *Hardwired to Connect: The New Scientific Case for Authoritative Communities*. The commission—made up of doctors, research scientists, and youth service professionals—described "recent scientific findings suggesting that children are biologically 'hardwired' for enduring attachments to other people and for moral and spiritual meaning."[1] Lack of enduring attachments is associated with children's depression, anxiety, attention deficit, conduct disorders, and thoughts of suicide.

What is true of children is also true of adults: God has hardwired all of us to connect, to create deep and lasting relationship. Science only discovers what God reveals in the Scriptures about His creation and its design.

Our objective for Week 2 is to understand more deeply that relationship is God's idea. However, sin has marred every human relationship and has left each of us with scars of varying severity. Some of us are deeply wounded and reluctant to get close to anyone. Others have patterns they have learned that keep them from having what God designed them to have—deep relationship. We need to understand this about ourselves and accept God's help to move past our broken behaviors and fears. If maturity is loving God and others well, then we need a complete understanding of the problem we humans face and what God has done to help us resolve it.

1. Commission on Children at Risk, *Hardwired to Connect: The New Scientific Case for Authoritative Communities*, YMCA, Institute for American Values, and Dartmouth Medical School, Broadway Publications, 2003.

Day 1: Hardwired to Connect

Many people read that we are created in the image of God (**Gen. 1:27**) and wonder what that means. Well, it means several things, one of which is that we are created to be in relationship.

God did not create us because He was lonely. He has never been lonely. He has been in relationship within the Trinity for all eternity. That is, God has eternally been three Persons with one undivided Essence. God has eternally been the Father loving and glorifying His Son, the Son loving and glorifying the Father, and the Holy Spirit loving and glorifying both Father and Son. He is one undivided God with relationship in His very essence. (If that's hard for you to wrap your mind around, consider that the God of the universe is more complicated than quantum physics, and physics alone is hard to understand.)

For our purposes today, the only thing you need to understand about the Trinity is that God has always been in loving relationships. He didn't create us so that He could receive love. He created us so that He could give us the overflow of the love He already had.

When the Lord created the world, at every turn He said it was good until the last day when He made the man. Then He said it was not good. What wasn't good—or complete—was that the man was alone.

However, the man wasn't utterly alone; he had a perfect relationship with God. Yet in God's eyes that wasn't enough. God knew that He had created the man to be in relationship with other humans. Some might say the man needed a wife, but that isn't quite it. The apostle Paul later wrote that it was better for some people to remain unmarried, as he was (1 Cor. 7:7–8), so not everyone needs a spouse. Not everyone needs children. However, from God's perspective, everyone needs close relationships not only with Him but with other humans as well.

Many Christians have a me-and-Jesus mentality. They think all they need is Jesus, and they keep everyone else at arm's length. But

So God created mankind in his own image, in the image of God he created them; male and female he created them. (Gen. 1:27)

God says that's not good. A relationship with Jesus is certainly essential for every person—we have a hole within us that only God can fill. However, God made us for more—relationships with other humans. Humans are designed to need relationships with physical and spiritual families.

1. Do you agree that it is not good for you to be alone—having a relationship with God but no close relationships with other believers? Why or why not?

   _____

   _____

   _____

The LORD God said, "It is not good for the man to be alone. I will make a helper suitable for him." (Gen. 2:18)

2. In **Genesis 2:18**, God says He will make the man a "helper suitable for him." A helper isn't necessarily a subordinate; elsewhere in the Old Testament, God is called our helper, using the same Hebrew word. In this verse, what sorts of help might God have had in mind?

   _____

   _____

   _____

3. What do relationships with others provide for you that you cannot get alone?

   _____

   _____

   _____

4. Do you feel like you're mostly getting what you need from other people, or are there some things you're not getting? What are those things?

   _____

   _____

   _____

5. Are you seeking to have the Lord help you give others what they need from you? What do you think God wants to give others through you?

   _____

   _____

   _____

Day 2: What Went Wrong?

In the Garden of Eden, we had a perfect world in every respect until a choice by a person with free will corrupted it. God gave Adam and Eve a choice, because relationship requires freedom to choose real alternatives with consequences. Love has to be freely chosen.

The Author of life is also the authority over His design. He gets to put a tree in the garden and say, "Don't eat from this. It will have bad consequences." This was an opportunity for Adam and Eve to choose trust and love (**Gen. 2:15–17**).

In the perfectly designed creation, Adam and Eve could be naked with each other, physically and emotionally, and feel no shame, no fear of being seen as inadequate or unlovable (**Gen. 2:25**). They had no conflict with each other and no attempts to manipulate the other or abuse their power. This is how relationships are supposed to be.

But something went wrong. The serpent (Satan) tempted Eve into sin, and Adam followed her example. They chose to doubt God's love and to disobey Him. They ate the forbidden fruit. And this sabotaged their relationships both with God and with each other.

If God is the source of relationship, the devil is the source of division. He knew that if he could contaminate Eve's trust in God by sowing doubt in her mind ("Did God really say . . . ?" and "You will not certainly die . . . you will be like God."), then her relationship with Adam and all future humans would be undermined. Satan questioned God's motives and got Eve to think that God was keeping something good from her for His own unloving purposes (**Gen. 3:1–7**).

As soon as Adam and Eve broke their relationship with God by disobeying Him, their sin also shattered their relationship with each other. They felt shame about their nakedness. They knew

The LORD God took the man and put him in the Garden of Eden to work it and take care of it. And the LORD God commanded the man, "You are free to eat from any tree in the garden; but you must not eat from the tree of the knowledge of good and evil, for when you eat from it you will certainly die." (Gen. 2:15–17)

Adam and his wife were both naked, and they felt no shame. (Gen. 2:25)

Now the serpent was more crafty than any of the wild animals the LORD God had made. He said to the woman, "Did God really say, 'You must not eat from any tree in the garden'?"

The woman said to the serpent, "We may eat fruit from the trees in the garden, but God did say, 'You must not eat fruit from the tree that is in the middle of the garden, and you must not touch it, or you will die.'"

"You will not certainly die," the serpent said to the woman. "For God knows that when you eat from it your

eyes will be opened, and you will be like God, knowing good and evil."

When the woman saw that the fruit of the tree was good for food and pleasing to the eye, and also desirable for gaining wisdom, she took some and ate it. She also gave some to her husband, who was with her, and he ate it. Then the eyes of both of them were opened, and they realized they were naked; so they sewed fig leaves together and made coverings for themselves. (Gen. 3:1–7)

they could be seen and found wanting. They wanted to hide from God and each other. When God came to find them, Adam blamed Eve for what had happened, and Eve blamed the devil. Neither of them was willing to take responsibility, so they were in conflict. And God predicted that the conflict would only get worse.

We were created for relationship, but sin has destroyed our ability to have what we were created to have. Instead of a garden, we live in a world with thorns (Gen. 3:18). Pleasurable gardening has given way to toil for survival (3:17). Marriage, childbearing, and child raising are painful (3:16). The war between the devil and humankind will be ongoing until the descendant of Eve (Jesus) crushes the serpent's head (3:15).

It's crucial that we understand what we were created for and what has gone wrong. When God is not accepted as the King He is, there can be no relationship with Him. When we choose ourselves as kings and make our own way, it separates us from God and others. I cannot trust you if you seek your own good over mine. Sin ruins relationship.

Pride poisons our relationship with God. Pride says, "I will not submit to you as King" and denies who God is. By refusing to submit to the Designer's authority, we always destroy what God intended. Pride also poisons our relationships with others, because we choose ourselves over them and use them rather than love them. By making ourselves the center of our relationships, we destroy them. When we compete with one another for who will sit on the throne in the relationship, neither ends up benefiting.

Yet we still long for relationships the way our bodies long for water. We need relationship to survive and thrive because God designed us to need it.

1. Read the excerpts from Genesis 2 and 3 above. How is the story of Adam and Eve your story also? Which parts do you identify with?

_____

_____

_____

2. Is pride affecting any of your relationships now? If so, how?

3. In what ways are you happy to submit to God as King?

4. In what ways do you resist submitting to God as King?

5. How has shame (the fear of being seen and known as a sinner, a failure, or inadequate) affected your relationships?

Day 3: The Father's Lost Children

When sin entered the world, all human relationships were broken. We inherit that brokenness at birth, and it dogs our steps throughout our lives. The devil told Eve a half-truth when he said eating the fruit wouldn't lead to death. It didn't lead immediately to physical death, but it did cause immediate relational death, and it set in motion the process of physical death. God knew what He was talking about.

We are like phones that stay charged as long as we are connected to the phone charger (God), but once separation between the phone and the charger occurs, we begin to run off our own battery. We run off our own understanding, which is limited to our own thoughts, our own feelings, our own desires. And our battery slowly dies.

Some ask why God would allow the world to continue once it was contaminated.

Jesus told a parable that reveals God's overall plan to save us. The story is called the Prodigal Son because *prodigal* is an old word meaning "wasteful." It's worth your time to read the parable in full in **Luke 15**.

1. In Luke 15, how was the relationship between the younger son and the father a broken relationship?

   _____

   _____

   _____

2. How was the relationship between the older son and the father also broken?

   _____

   _____

   _____

There was a man who had two sons. The younger one said to his father, "Father, give me my share of the estate." So he divided his property between them.

Not long after that, the younger son got together all he had, set off for a distant country and there squandered his wealth in wild living. After he had spent everything, there was a severe famine in that whole country, and he began to be in need. So he went and hired himself out to a citizen of that

46

3. How was the relationship between the two brothers broken?

_____

_____

_____

4. The father in the story is, of course, a picture of our Father God. What hope for the healing of relationships does the story offer?

_____

_____

_____

God has done what Jesus describes in the story. He has allowed us to go into a world of our making so we could discover that all of it leads to pig slop. He did this because He is a God of relationships, and relationships require choices. He chooses us, but we must choose Him too. God allows us to take our portion of His wealth and go off to a far country and squander it. He allows this, yet He waits for us to return home. (Unlike in the story, He whispers, "Come home" to us through creation, other believers, and directly into our hearts, even while we are lost.) Then when He glimpses us, He runs to us. He longs to restore relationship. In fact, even before we think about returning, He orchestrates what happens in the world in order to draw us back. He doesn't cause sin, but He allows it in hopes that as we experience the broken world sin creates, we will decide that God the Father was right all along—we will come to our senses and go home.

And even those of us who seemingly stay home with God can still miss His heart. The older brother is furious with his father because he doesn't give his brother what he thinks the brother deserves. He feels he has been his father's slave, even though all he has comes from a generous father who didn't have to give him anything. He lacks love for his brother. Notice that the father's heart is to get the older son to come into the house and celebrate with the family, including the younger son. The father wants the two brothers in relationship. Likewise, our God wants to restore our relationships with Himself through what He has done in

country, who sent him to his fields to feed pigs. He longed to fill his stomach with the pods that the pigs were eating, but no one gave him anything.

When he came to his senses, he said, "How many of my father's hired servants have food to spare, and here I am starving to death! I will set out and go back to my father and say to him: Father, I have sinned against heaven and against you. I am no longer worthy to be called your son; make me like one of your hired servants." So he got up and went to his father.

But while he was still a long way off, his father saw him and was filled with compassion for him; he ran to his son, threw his arms around him and kissed him.

The son said to him, "Father, I have sinned against heaven and against you. I am no longer worthy to be called your son."

But the father said to his servants, "Quick! Bring the best robe and put it on him. Put a ring on his finger and sandals on his feet. Bring the fattened calf and kill it. Let's have a feast and celebrate. For this son of mine was dead and is alive again; he was lost and is found." So they began to celebrate.

Meanwhile, the older son was in the field. When he came near the house, he heard music and dancing. So he called one of the servants and asked him what was going on. "Your brother *has come," he replied, "and your father has killed the fattened calf because he has him back safe and sound."*

The older brother became angry and refused to go in. So his father went out and pleaded with him. But he answered his father, "Look! All these years I've been slaving for you and never disobeyed your orders. Yet you never gave me even a young goat so I could celebrate with my friends. But when this son of yours who has squandered your property with prostitutes comes home, you kill the fattened calf for him!"

"My son," the father said, "you are always with me, and everything I have is yours. But we had to celebrate and be glad, because this brother of yours was dead and is alive again; he was lost and is found." (Luke 15:11–32)

Christ, and He also wants to restore our relationships with one another.

5. How has God pursued you for restoration?

_____

_____

_____

6. What do you want to say to God about that?

_____

_____

_____

7. Do you have any brothers or sisters with whom your relationship is still broken? You don't have to name them to your group if confidentiality is important, but do take a moment to think about whether there is someone with whom you need to reconcile and celebrate.

_____

_____

_____

Day 4: Resurrection Power

In **Ephesians 1:18–20**, Paul prays that we will know the hope to which God has called us. That hope is for complete restoration after we die, and it is also hope for here and now. His incomparably great power—the power that raised Jesus from the dead—is already at work in us who believe. God will raise us from the dead after we die, and He also raises things here and now that are dead because of sin. Our broken ability and the healing we need to have healthy (not perfect) relationships can be restored by the resurrection power of God.

I pray that the eyes of your heart may be enlightened in order that you may know the hope to which he has called you, the riches of his glorious inheritance in his holy people, and his incomparably great power for us who believe. That power is the same as the mighty strength he exerted when he raised Christ from the dead and seated him at his right hand in the heavenly realms. (Eph. 1:18–20)

1. Does your hope of resurrection in the future affect the way you deal with things now? How? Or why not?

   _____

   _____

   _____

2. How do you think our hope of resurrection is supposed to affect the way we deal with things now?

   _____

   _____

   _____

God is the great reconciler. He humbled Himself in obedience, even to death on the cross (Phil. 2:7–8), and gave us what we needed rather than what we deserved. In **2 Corinthians**, Paul speaks of reconciliation between us and God. This is crucial—in order to have healthy relationships with one another, we need to build on the foundation of a solidly reconciled relationship with God.

God the Son came as a servant and a sacrifice to bridge the gap of separation between us and the Father. While we were God's enemies, He came for us. He gave us His Word and the Holy Spirit so that we can understand what love is. He does His work

All this is from God, who reconciled us to himself through Christ and gave us the ministry of reconciliation: that God was reconciling the world to himself in Christ, not counting people's sins against them. And he has committed to us the message of reconciliation. We are therefore Christ's

ambassadors, as though God were making his appeal through us. We implore you on Christ's behalf: Be reconciled to God. (2 Cor. 5:18–20)

This is the message we have heard from him and declare to you: God is light; in him there is no darkness at all. If we claim to have fellowship with him and yet walk in the darkness, we lie and do not live out the truth. But if we walk in the light, as he is in the light, we have fellowship with one another, and the blood of Jesus, his Son, purifies us from all sin.

If we claim to be without sin, we deceive ourselves and the truth is not in us. If we confess our sins, he is faithful and just and will forgive us our sins and purify us from all unrighteousness. (1 John 1:5–9)

through people as He changes them so that we can have tangible relationships to support, encourage, and even challenge us to walk with God.

The word "fellowship" in 1 John 1:7 is *koinonia*, which means communion, common life, partnership, community. In order to have community with other people, we need to "walk in the light."

3. Read **1 John 1:5–9**. What do you think it means to walk in the light? What behaviors and attitudes are involved?

_____

_____

_____

_____

_____

4. Do you have any relationships that are broken and need healing? Name them, even if you don't think there's anything you can do or want to do about them. You don't have to share these names with your group.

_____

_____

_____

5. Maybe you can't be brought back together with someone you named in question 4 because they need to do their part and you have no control over that. Or you may not be able to locate them, or they may have passed away. But you can pray for resurrection power to heal you in this loss and enable you to do your part in acknowledging any fault on your side and seeking God's forgiveness. What is your part that is under your control? For example, is there any sin you need to confess to God? How can you walk in the light with regard to this situation?

_____

_____

_____

_____

6. Without naming the person to your group (no gossip), what steps can you take to seek to restore the relationship? Look at **Matthew 18:15–17** for ideas, and allow your group to hold you accountable to the plan.

_____

_____

_____

_____

_____

If your brother or sister sins, go and point out their fault, just between the two of you. If they listen to you, you have won them over. But if they will not listen, take one or two others along, so that "every matter may be established by the testimony of two or three witnesses." If they still refuse to listen, tell it to the church; and if they refuse to listen even to the church, treat them as you would a pagan or a tax collector. (Matt. 18:15–17)

Day 5: All the Law and the Prophets

Hearing that Jesus had silenced the Sadducees, the Pharisees got together. One of them, an expert in the law, tested him with this question: "Teacher, which is the greatest commandment in the Law?"

Jesus replied: "'Love the Lord your God with all your heart and with all your soul and with all your mind.' This is the first and greatest commandment. And the second is like it: 'Love your neighbor as yourself.' All the Law and the Prophets hang on these two commandments." (Matt. 22:34–40)

God has always been a God of relationship. When He gave the law of Moses to Israel, the laws were designed to strengthen and protect relationships with God and others. Jesus said the two greatest commandments in the law—the ones that summed up the whole law—were to love God with all your being and to love your neighbor as yourself (**Matt. 22:34–40**). The first four of the Ten Commandments deal with loving God, and the last six deal with loving our neighbor (Exod. 20:1–17).

All of the rules God has ever made have been designed to help us love Him and others well. They are meant for the promotion or protection of relationship. Rules are not meant to be ways we prove ourselves better than others and good enough for God. Rather, obeying God is a loving response to His offer of relationship. To seek status by obedience is to tragically miss the point.

God's kingdom is one of relationship lost and restored. The Scriptures tell us that in the end we will be in a new heaven and a new earth, where we will live in close relationship with God and with people from every tribe and tongue and nation. All the enemies of relationship will be destroyed (Rev. 7:9–10; 21:1–8).

1. Have you ever tried to earn God's approval by obedience to rules? If so, what was that experience like for you? If you have never tried this, describe someone else you've seen who has tried this.

   _____

   _____

   _____

2. How does it affect you to think of God's commands as being designed to promote or protect relationships? How does it affect your attitude toward His commands?

_____
_____
_____
_____

3. What opportunities have you had this week to love God with all your heart, soul, and mind? What challenges do you face that will test your love for God in the coming week?

_____
_____
_____
_____

4. What opportunities have you had this week to love your neighbor? What challenges do you face that will test your love for a neighbor, a friend, a co-worker in the coming week?

_____
_____
_____
_____

Again many think of Christianity as just a relationship with God. They have a me-and-Jesus mentality. However, this is distorted. Our team at Real Life Ministries (RLM) often works with the staff of a whole church at one time. They often come to us to learn a new strategy to make disciples and grow the church. But before we talk about strategy, we help them identify places where what they already have is out of relational alignment. Many times there are unresolved issues between the leaders—secret bitterness, anger, and hurt that they refuse to deal with. Everyone on the staff feels the tension between those who are supposed to be on the same team, the same family of believers. However, they let it continue and, instead, want to focus on learning new growth strategies. We often put our meeting on hold to help them deal with unresolved conflicts and have them read what Jesus said in **Matthew 5:23–24.** We ask them why God would want to add more people to a group that is already poisoned by bitterness at the highest level.

So if you are offering your gift at the altar and there remember that your brother has something against you, leave your gift there before the altar and go. First be reconciled to your brother, and then come and offer your gift. (Matt. 5:23–24 ESV)

53

Likewise, husbands, live with your wives in an understanding way, show-ing honor to the woman as the weaker vessel, since they are heirs with you of the grace of life, so that your prayers may not be hindered. (1 Pet. 3:7 ESV)

You see, how you respond to God's other children affects how God uses and blesses you. We see this in the church and in the home, especially between husbands and wives (**1 Pet. 3:7**).

5. Is there any place in your life where the devil has been al-lowed to build a stronghold of bitterness that is affecting your relationships with other believers? Without gossiping, allow your group to help you deal with this.

_____

_____

_____

_____

6. What are the key insights you have had in Week 2 of this study? What do you want to take from this week and apply to your life?

_____

_____

_____

_____

_____

Growing Together

Day 1: Discuss question 1. There are two ways we can detect immaturity in ourselves: if we are unwilling to admit we have needs, or we have a demanding attitude that expects the group to revolve itself around us and our needs. As mature people, we can voice needs without demanding that others respond, and as we listen to others share, we think about how we can help respond to their needs. In this light, discuss questions 3 and 4.

Day 2: Discuss question 1, which part of Adam and Eve's story you might identify with.

Day 3: The Prodigal Son is a story that all of us can relate to in some way: the father, the brother, or the prodigal. Discuss which of the three best illustrates you; you might see yourself in more than one role.

Day 4: Discuss question 2. Share some life stories of restored relationships. With the name(s) from question 4 in mind, discuss question 6, what steps to take toward restoration in these relationships.

Day 5: Share your challenges from questions 3 and 4. Have another group member write down a KEYWORD as a REMINDER for your answer on Week 3's Growing Together page (p. 74) so the group can check in with each member next week about how it went. This kind of gentle, nonjudgmental accountability can help you grow.

Check in on the accountability requests from Week 1.

Pray for those on Week 1's prayer list.

Week 3

Love Is Spiritual Maturity

Some time ago a man who was considering joining our church asked to meet with me. He had a great deal of Bible training, believed he had the gift of teaching, and wanted to be able to teach our people. Teachers in our church have to be spiritually mature, so I asked him a series of questions to assess his level of spiritual maturity. I asked him why he had left his previous churches, whether he had any deep relationships with other believers, and whether he was accountable to anyone. He said he had left seven churches in five years because of disagreements with the leaderships of those churches. His only deep relationship was with his wife, and he considered that to be sufficient. He was not interested in joining one of our home groups. He was accountable to no one but God, he said.

To him, spiritual maturity meant extensive Bible knowledge. But while we see knowledge of the Bible and an ability to impart it to others as important, it isn't enough at our church. We believe spiritual maturity also requires the ability to love God and others well. It requires deep relationships. This week, you'll see why we see maturity that way.

Day 1: Resounding Gongs

We grow to maturity best if we are in relationship with others. And there's a big reason for that: the goal that we call maturity is the consistent habit of loving God and loving others well. It is not simply knowing the Bible well (although that helps). It's not laboring on five church committees (although service is a form of love, if done for the right reasons). Maturity is loving well and allowing others to love us well too.

We saw last week that loving God and others sums up the Old Testament law. It also sums up what the New Testament asks of us. Consider the **four passages** in the margin.

1. How does each of these passages hold up love as the summation of what God expects of us?

   • John 13:34–35

   _____

   _____

   • Matthew 5:44–46

   _____

   _____

   • Galatians 5:6

   _____

   _____

   • 1 Corinthians 13:1–3

   _____

   _____

   _____

Paul tells us in 1 Corinthians that the Corinthian church had great teachers and supernatural giftings, yet the leaders and the

[Jesus said,] "A new command I give you: Love one another. As I have loved you, so you must love one another. By this everyone will know that you are my disciples, if you love one another." (John 13:34–35)

[Jesus said,] "But I tell you, love your enemies and pray for those who persecute you, that you may be children of your Father in heaven. He causes his sun to rise on the evil and the good, and sends rain on the righteous and the unrighteous. If you love those who love you, what reward will you get? Are not even the tax collectors doing that?" (Matt. 5:44–46)

For in Christ Jesus neither circumcision nor uncircumcision has any value. The only thing that counts is faith expressing itself through love. (Gal. 5:6)

If I speak in the tongues of men or of angels, but do not have love, I am only a resounding gong or a clanging cymbal. If I have the gift of prophecy and can fathom all mysteries and all knowledge, and if I have a faith that can move mountains, but do not have love, I am nothing. If I give all I possess to the poor and give over my body to hardship that I may boast, but do not have love, I gain nothing. (1 Cor. 13:1–3)

people were mere infants because they fought with one another. He wanted them to excel in love. And he said they could know mysteries (knowledge), speak in the tongues of angels (spiritual gifts), give their money away and die as martyrs (follow the rules) but still be immature if they lacked love.

This immaturity makes believers destructive to themselves and others. It creates people who are missing the crucial component of God's love while they declare to a lost world that they have found what they need for abundant life. It doesn't take long for the world to see the disconnect.

Paul's point is not that we shouldn't seek knowledge or giftings or generosity with money. Those are all good things. His point is that we need to do all those things because we love—not because we want to earn salvation or respect. We are hardwired to connect, so we can't settle for a relationship with God that lacks the essential dimension of relationship with others.

This is why discipleship has to happen in relationship. We learn to be relational by relating. We grow mature in love by seeing love modeled for us and by practicing love.

2. Describe what it would look like in behavior and attitude to love others the way Jesus loves us (John 13:34). Apply this to a person or situation in your own life.

_____

_____

_____

_____

_____

3. Describe what you think it would look like in behavior and attitude to love your enemies (Matt. 5:44). Again, apply this in your own life. Why does that take maturity?

_____

_____

_____

_____

_____

4. Is it a new idea for you to think about spiritual maturity in terms of loving God and loving others? What are some other measures of maturity that you have seen people use?

_____

_____

_____

_____

_____

5. "This immaturity [lack of love] makes believers destructive to themselves and others." Have you seen this to be true? If so, how?

_____

_____

_____

_____

_____

Day 2: What Love Really Means

But the fruit of the Spirit is love, joy, peace, forbearance, kindness, goodness, faithfulness, gentleness and self-control. Against such things there is no law. (Gal. 5:22–23)

Love is patient, love is kind. It does not envy, it does not boast, it is not proud. It does not dishonor others, it is not self-seeking, it is not easily angered, it keeps no record of wrongs. Love does not delight in evil but rejoices with the truth. It always protects, always trusts, always hopes, always perseveres.

Love never fails. (1 Cor. 13:4–8)

Love is an overused word today. We can love ice cream or be in love with someone we hardly know. So Paul went to the trouble of defining it for two communities he was writing to.

Because we have a relationship with the Father through Jesus the Son, we have been given the indwelling of the Holy Spirit, and He begins to produce in us the fruit of the Spirit. This fruit, defined in **Galatians 5**, is all about relationship. Love for whom? Forbearance toward whom? Kindness toward whom? It is a picture of mature relationships.

And then in **1 Corinthians 13**, Paul spells out a definition that takes the word *love* back from the devil, who stole it and sold a cheap imitation to our culture. Love is patient—it doesn't lose its temper. Love is kind—it seeks the good of the other, and does no harm. The love in pop songs is self-centered, aiming at one's own gratification, but Paul's picture of love is benevolent and laced with commitment and grace. It is a choice, not a feeling, and yet it is warmhearted and capable of feeling. It is self-sacrificing, the way Jesus underwent terrible suffering and death for us. Love is choosing to lay down our lives for another.

As we grow up into our salvation, we move from self-centeredness to other-centeredness, from consumer to contributor, not because we think less of ourselves but because we think of ourselves less often. Most Christians use the word "I" and "me" a lot—I don't like the music; I didn't like the preaching; they didn't welcome me at church; they didn't notice I was gone; they don't have the program I wanted; I don't feel the way I used to feel about them anymore; I love him but I'm not in love with him; he doesn't make me feel the way he used to. These statements say that others exist for us—a far cry from what love would say. We need to grow out of this attitude.

The churches Paul worked with were full of people with different convictions, preferences, and social statuses. Some liked

Paul's teaching, while others liked that of another teacher named Apollos. Some thought they should stick to kosher food, while others thought all food was clean for Christians. They had different convictions about keeping the Sabbath. Instead of arguing about these things or dividing into separate fellowships depending on their convictions, Paul urged the believers in a city to stick together. He wanted the whole diverse mix to bring their gifts and ideas together and demonstrate unity to outsiders. He wanted believers to care more about each other than about their opinions. I believe that attitude should still prevail in churches today. There should be very few reasons to split a church or leave a church.

1. Which statement about love in 1 Corinthians 13:4–8 do you most want to grow in? Why that one?

2. Up to now, have you been more of a consumer (expecting only to receive) or more of a contributor in your church? What's the evidence?

3. Where do you see diversity in your church? Does it tend to cause arguments or fruitful collaboration? Describe how.

4. How can members of congregations love their leaders even when their leaders aren't perfect?

5. For the next day or two, pay attention to how often you use the words "I" and "me" in conversation or inner thoughts. What did you learn?

_____

_____

_____

Day 3: Love Forgives and Endures

Often when people know that sin has hurt their relationships, they are afraid to trust again. Yet Paul's definition of love in 1 Corinthians 13 tells us that love keeps no record of wrongs. In other words, it forgives. It also tells us that love endures all things—it keeps trying to make the relationship work. When others fail us, love offers grace.

Our love must be like this, because until Jesus returns and eliminates the devil, our sinful natures, and our confusion and ignorance, we will all make mistakes. So grace must be given and received. The only way broken people can have real relationship is if forgiveness is a part of our lives.

Jesus tells us to reconcile a broken relationship before we bring our gifts to the altar (**Matt. 5:23–24**). If we're not okay with other people, we're not okay with God.

Harboring unforgiveness is like driving a car with your eyes fixed on the rearview mirror. A crash with harm to others and yourself is inevitable.

Of course, we need to be wise in choosing friends. Not everyone is trustworthy. And if someone has an addiction or other harmful habit, there is a time to confront them and draw a boundary for their own good. This is the loving thing to do. But even when we say no to them and insist that they get help, we need to do it in the spirit of seeking their highest good, not out of retaliation. And if the relationship needs to be distanced because they refuse to get help, this too is a loving choice. It shouldn't leave us stuck with a fear of ever trusting anyone again. It can take time to heal from a hurtful relationship, yet healing happens best if we move toward relationships with other people.

Read **Matthew 18:21–22**. Why are we to be so generous with forgiveness? Because God is that generous with us. Jesus told Peter to forgive that often because He wanted us to become more and more like Him—He forgives us that often. He forgives us over and

[Jesus said,] "Therefore, if you are offering your gift at the altar and there remember that your brother or sister has something against you, leave your gift there in front of the altar. First go and be reconciled to them; then come and offer your gift." (Matt. 5:23–24)

Then Peter came to Jesus and asked, "Lord, how many times shall I forgive my brother or sister who sins against me? Up to seven times?"

Jesus answered, "I tell you, not seven times, but seventy-seven times." (Matt. 18:21–22)

over and over, often for the very same sin. The more aware we are of our own failings and God's forgiveness, the more we are humbled and grateful, so we persevere in the same way with others.

1. How do you respond to the idea of forgiving someone over and over for the same fault? What are the risks and costs associated with this?

_____

_____

_____

2. What are the benefits of persistent forgiveness? Or put another way, what are the costs of not persistently forgiving?

_____

_____

_____

3. Suppose someone has a habit of belittling you in front of other people. How can you handle this in the most loving way? What if the person is a member of your church? What if the person is your spouse?

_____

_____

_____

_____

_____

4. Suppose your friend is on the elder board of your church. Your friend has a serious disagreement with your pastor, and your pastor asks your friend to resign from the board. You agree with your friend about the matter under dispute. Your friend resigns from the board and leaves the church. What do you feel? What do you do? Why?

_____

_____

_____

_____

_____

Day 4: Context Is Everything

Recently I met with a couple who had tried out a dozen different churches in our area and even had been members of some for many years before coming to us. They weren't happy with any of the churches nor particularly happy with us either. But at least they were willing to come and talk about it. I discovered that they had been married for more than fifty years, which is commendable. So I asked them, "As spouses, have you ever disagreed with each other over the course of your marriage?"

They both nodded and said, "Sure."

I continued. "What did you do then, when you disagreed with each other?"

"Well," said the husband, "we prayed for each other, and we talked it out." He said he had to go to Scripture over and over again at times to wash the world's way of doing things out of his mind. The wife agreed. As they talked about how to make a marriage work, they shared both frustrating times and peaceful times that resulted from sticking it out, all the while quoting portions of 1 Corinthians 13 that had helped them define what God wanted in a marriage. I asked what issues they had begun disagreeing on and how they ended up coming to their resolutions. I asked them if they still had to accept things about each other after all these years that they wish they could have changed. Of course the answer was a humorous yes as they looked at each other.

I asked a follow-up question. "In the midst of any of your disagreements, did you ever wonder if the grass was greener elsewhere? Were you ever tempted to leave your spouse for someone else?"

They both chuckled. The wife answered first. "I would never let my mind go there. I was committed to him for life."

The husband said, "We came to understand that the grass is never truly greener. It only sometimes looks that way. But every husband and wife disagree sometimes, same as us. We chose to love each other for better or worse—we had made a commitment."

"So let me ask you a final question," I said. "You've applied biblical truth and principles about marriage to your lives so well. You have talked about forgiveness and confronting and looking past issues. But you know that the Scriptures give us so much guidance about how to act in the family of God too. So why haven't you applied Scripture to your dealings with people in your spiritual family at church the way you have in your marriage?" They both silently looked at me and let the question sink in.

I encouraged them to read together through Ephesians 4–5. Chapter 4 deals with unity and maturity in the body of Christ. Chapter 5 compares this picture to marriage. In fact, this powerful verse, Ephesians 5:21, "Submit to one another out of reverence for Christ," comes in the overall foundational context of Ephesians 4:3, "Make every effort to keep the unity of the Spirit through the bond of peace." As spouses, we want to be committed to each other for better or worse. As Christians, we need the same level of commitment to our church families.

You see, many like to use the Scriptures meant for the context of the church in the context of marriage instead, and I think this is a huge mistake. First Corinthians 13, which is read at many marriage ceremonies and may be important for marriage, is about the church, according to the writer—Paul, inspired by the Holy Spirit. Often we forget that relationship in the church is to be so close that it can be termed *family*. So many people who are deemed mature fail to have the kind of relationships described here with anyone other than their spouse and thus completely miss the intent of these passages. We are called to weave the 1 Corinthians 13 kind of love into our relationships with other believers.

A woman in our home group recently described to us how she continually takes 1 Corinthians 13 and puts our names and faces behind each directive, asking herself questions along the way. *Am I being patient with Jim? Am I being kind to Jim?*

That's exactly what we all need to do with those we are called to love. Are we truly loving people the way Jesus wants us to love?

1. How do you respond to the idea that you should be as committed to your church as you are to your marriage? (Or if you are single, as committed as you would be to a marriage.) Does that seem like a reasonable reading of **1 Corinthians 13:4–8** and **Ephesians 4:1–6**? Why or why not?

2. Suppose you have been attending a church for some years. The format of the weekend service changes in ways you don't like. What do you do? Why?

3. Suppose you are in a home group and one of the other members is persistently critical of you and your spouse. What do you do? Why?

Love is patient, love is kind. It does not envy, it does not boast, it is not proud. It does not dishonor others, it is not self-seeking, it is not easily angered, it keeps no record of wrongs. Love does not delight in evil but rejoices with the truth. It always protects, always trusts, always hopes, always perseveres.

Love never fails. (1 Cor. 13:4–8)

As a prisoner for the Lord, then, I urge you to live a life worthy of the calling you have received. Be completely humble and gentle; be patient, bearing with one another in love. Make every effort to keep the unity of the Spirit through the bond of peace. There is one body and one Spirit, just as you were called to one hope when you were called; one Lord, one faith, one baptism; one God and Father of all, who is over all and through all and in all. (Eph. 4:1–6)

Day 5: Learning to Feed Yourself

It's hard enough to stay committed in a marriage. It's even harder to stay committed to a church where you're dealing with the personalities of not just one person but many. Many may not be mature at loving others or even have a desire to become so. How is it possible to deal with the pain that can come from such relationships?

The kind of love Paul calls for in 1 Corinthians 13 isn't human; it's supernatural. God has given us some tools that can help us live out this kind of love.

First, we have a model to study: Jesus. We can treat Him as our ultimate role model and watch how He treats people.

Second, we have the Word of God as the Holy Spirit–inspired road map that tells us where to go and how to get there.

Third, we have the Holy Spirit living inside us. He empowers us to live out what we have learned in the Word of God. His fruit is love, joy, peace, and so on. We need to abide or remain in Jesus through the Holy Spirit the way a branch abides or remains in a vine (**John 15:1–2, 4–6**).

Fourth, hopefully we have some human models to emulate. Ideally we were given godly parents to help us see what love looks like in practice, and we have pastors and teachers who model what we read about in Scripture. Paul said, "Follow my example, as I follow the example of Christ" (1 Cor. 11:1). We can see in the New Testament how Paul does things and imitate him. And ideally again, we have human leaders in a church and at home who are good role models.

Fifth, we have the Holy Spirit working through other people as we do life together with them. As they walk with Jesus in His Word, they make themselves available to God to speak into our lives. They encourage and exhort us, and we encourage and exhort them too. Together we remain in Christ and bear much fruit.

I am the true vine, and my Father is the gardener. He cuts off every branch in me that bears no fruit, while every branch that does bear fruit he prunes so that it will be even more fruitful. . . . Remain in me, as I also remain in you. No branch can bear fruit by itself; it must remain in the vine. Neither can you bear fruit unless you remain in me.

I am the vine; you are the branches. If you remain in me and I in you, you will bear much fruit; apart from me you can do nothing. If you do not remain in me, you are like a branch

Gradually we mature, moving from consumers to contributors. We no longer expect the weekend service and home group alone to feed us, because we are learning to feed ourselves through time alone with Jesus each day, through Christian books, and through listening to sermons and Christian music during the week. As we spend time with other believers in daily relationships, we are fed as God works through them in our lives. We move from being takers to being sharers of the responsibility with others to feed one another. (See **1 John 1:7**).

that is thrown away and withers; such branches are picked up, thrown into the fire and burned. (John 15:1–2, 4–6)

We learn to see the weekend service through others' eyes. We may not like the topic being preached on, but we recognize that it may be for others this week. We pray for those who are listening. We may not like the style of music, but we recognize that there are older or younger believers who love it, and we are glad they are worshiping with it. We look for the people coming to the service who need a hug or a listening ear. We even volunteer to serve in the children's ministry so that parents can be fed in the service and kids can be loved by the spiritual community.

If we walk in the light, as he is in the light, we have fellowship with one another, and the blood of Jesus, his Son, purifies us from all sin. (1 John 1:7)

In the same way, we move from seeing the home group or the men's or women's group being about how we are fed to being about how we can feed others as well. We make sure we are learning to feed ourselves in many ways so that when we meet with other believers, we are not limping in, starved to death because of personal neglect of our spirits.

1. According to the text above, how does a Christian feed himself or herself?

   _____

   _____

   _____

2. Do you know how to feed yourself? If so, are you making the time to do it? If you don't know how, how could you learn? Who could help you?

   _____

   _____

   _____

3. How do you go about abiding or remaining in Jesus like a branch in a vine? What does this involve in practical terms? If you don't know, how could you find out?

_____

_____

_____

_____

4. What would you tell a person who says his life is too busy right now to feed himself, and he just needs to be able to show up each week at a church that feeds him?

_____

_____

_____

_____

The other day I had a man come to me to say he was leaving our church because we did not always preach verse-by-verse sermons. I told him I liked verse by verse too and would listen to Christian preachers on the radio who used that style a couple of times a week. I told him I read Scripture verse by verse every day. I reminded him that if you planned on feeding yourself once a week with only the kind of food you like physically, you would have little energy to fight off sickness or work for a living. I told him that a church is much more than just the sermon on Sunday and that a healthy believer will read Scripture daily, listen to good sermons in the car or on the internet, read good Christian books filled with spiritual teaching, have great talks with other believers, and engage in relationships that encourage and protect both themselves and others. As you grow, you move from expecting church to be built around your own preferences to being a contributor who seeks to hear from God's Word in whatever style is preached. The Holy Spirit can work in many ways when He is invited into what is happening. Worship isn't about your preference of music; it's about worshiping God and caring about His preference. His preference is that our hearts are about bringing glory to Him and caring for others in the room.

5. What would you say to this person?

_____

_____

_____

_____

6. What are the key insights you have had in Week 3 of this study? What do you want to take from this week and apply to your life?

_____

_____

_____

_____

Growing Together

Day 1: If there is someone in your life with whom you don't get along, share the situation with your group without naming names. Ask for guidance or even just prayer to support you in treating this person with love.

Day 2: Share your answers for question 1. Now might be a good time to check in briefly on group members' challenges from Week 2 (KEYWORD REMINDER below).

Days 3/4: Days 3 and 4 both have "suppose" questions for you to wrestle with. These have no easy answers, especially when the other person in the situation isn't relationally mature. Take a moment to skim through the scenarios and choose a few to toss out to the group. Wrestle together to come up with some mature responses. (Scenarios like these, worked out in role-playing, have played a big part in preparing us for situations we have eventually faced at RLM.)

Day 5: Discuss responses to questions 2 and 3. Share some key insights from the week.

Check in on the accountability requests from Week 1.

Pray for those on Week 1's prayer list.

KEYWORD REMINDER for member challenges from Week 2:
Name:

_____

Keyword:

_____

_____

Week 4

Family Matters

We saw in Week 1 that when people are born again at salvation, they automatically receive the spiritual DNA to grow from spiritual infancy into disciple-makers or spiritual parents (two names for the same function). There's more to the spiritual DNA than that, though. When we are born again at salvation, we are also born into a spiritual family. Not only do we have a heavenly Father, but we also have spiritual "sub-parents," the people who led us to Christ and have a responsibility to help us grow up in knowledge and obedience that expresses itself in love. And we have spiritual brothers and sisters with whom we have a bond, just as healthy natural siblings have. (In many cases these relationships are far healthier than blood relationships.) We are the household of God, all children together of our Father.

The objective for this week is to learn how to be a spiritual family with your brothers and sisters. If that sounds scary, given the people who go to your church, don't panic. Read on.

Day 1: The Bride of Christ—Part 1

When I gave my life to Christ, I told my dad that I would accept Jesus but I would never accept the church. I had been hurt by it and saw it as a losing team who didn't mind losing. I also saw it as fake, because people called you brother or sister but they didn't act like a family—at least not a functional one.

A few days later, my dad called me to ask a question about a situation he was dealing with in his church. (He was a pastor in a different town.) He told me that there was a family who really liked him but didn't like my mother. They wanted him to come to dinner but didn't want Mom to come. He asked me what he should do.

I was appalled—how could anyone not like my mother? I told him that he could not do it—if they didn't want Mom, then they couldn't have him either. You are one when you get married, and there was no way that they were asking him to do something good.

He paused and then I realized he had set the hook. He told me it's the same with Jesus—the church is the bride of Christ and you couldn't say you love the Groom and not accept the bride. We are called to be the bride and to love the bride. God loves His bride and expects us to be a part of it and love it as well (**2 Cor. 11:2; Rev. 19:7**).

The best way to love your spouse is to love your kids, and the best way to love your kids is to love your spouse. This is true in the church as well—the best way to love our Father is to love His children, our brothers and sisters. And the best way to love Jesus the Bridegroom is to love His church.

We are part of the household of God; we belong to our spiritual Father (**Eph. 2:19**). As our Father, He is to be obeyed, and every command He gives protects and promotes relationship. To obey God is to love Him; to obey Him by loving others is to love Him.

I am jealous for you with a godly jealousy. I promised you to one husband, to Christ, so that I might present you as a pure virgin to him. (2 Cor. 11:2)

*Let us rejoice and be glad
    and give him glory!
For the wedding of the Lamb has come,
    and his bride has made herself
        ready. (Rev. 19:7)*

Consequently, you are no longer foreigners and strangers, but fellow citizens with God's people and also members of his household. (Eph. 2:19)

If you have children, do you want your children to love and protect each other? If your older son or daughter did not care for the younger siblings after you had taught them to, would you be happy with them? Would you consider them mature?

1. Which of these arguments for loving your spiritual brothers and sisters do you find compelling, if any? Why?

   _____

   _____

   _____

2. What does a godly family look like?

   _____

   _____

   _____

3. Have you been resistant up to now to get close to your spiritual brothers and sisters, let them know the real you, and take an interest in who they really are? If so, why?

   _____

   _____

   _____

4. Have you been hurt by your natural family or your spiritual family? If so, how does that affect the way you are relating to your spiritual family now?

   _____

   _____

   _____

5. If past hurts are affecting present relationships, who can you talk with about those past hurts? Ironically, bringing those hurts out in the open with someone is the best way to heal them.

   _____

   _____

   _____

Day 2: The Bride of Christ—Part 2

I am the pastor of a church. Suppose my wife comes to church, but as she gets out of the car she tears a gaping hole in her dress and exposes herself to everyone who looks. But she doesn't know it. As she walks into the church, some people notice the hole but do nothing except snicker and point behind her back. Some come up to her and make a joke about it and laugh and embarrass her. Some just keep it to themselves and figure it's her problem. Or maybe they decide not to go to church anymore because of how careless the pastor's wife is. As her husband, how do I feel about those people when I hear about it? If they loved me and cared about what I cared about—my wife—they would not have scorned her, embarrassed her, or done nothing.

But what if a person walks up to her, takes off his coat without anyone noticing, and whispers in her ear that she had torn her dress and gently places the coat around her waist—no fanfare, just quiet and kind consideration so that my wife can walk to the bathroom without anyone noticing? How do I feel about that man? I would thank that man for respecting my wife and me enough to care for her.

This is what God calls us to do when we are a part of God's family. It's not enough to tolerate His bride. He wants so much more.

So many see the church's failings and refuse to see the need as an opportunity to minister to Christ's bride. Many see the broken church, full of people who fail, and they choose to avoid her. They shake their heads in disgust. They judge and mock. They either stay and criticize or leave and feel justified. That's no way to love God's bride.

If we want to love God best, we will bear with His bride's problems. Rather than expose the issues to the world, we will seek to be a part of the solution. Being a contributor rather than a consumer means we look for ways to help the bride be what God designed her to be.

God does not give us the right to leave. Paul tells us to bear with one another's faults (**Eph. 4:2**). As we grow up in the faith, we become easier to deal with, for sure. As we grow up, we also become more and more tolerant of others' mistakes. We recognize our own faults and God's constant grace toward us, and we become givers of grace.

Always be humble and gentle. Be patient with each other, making allowance for each other's faults because of your love. (Eph. 4:2 NLT)

We bear with the faults of those in the body much like a parent who sees her kids' problems but loves them anyway. She works to help them overcome their issues, and she also looks past their issues and sees their potential—how they can contribute to the family.

Jesus said, "Blessed are the peacemakers" (**Matt. 5:9**), which means that when we see a smoldering fire, we go to put it out rather than dumping gas on it. We see a hole in the fabric, and instead of just pointing it out, we recognize that God has revealed it to us so that we can meet that need.

God blesses those who work for peace, for they will be called the children of God. (Matt. 5:9 NLT)

1. What has your attitude been toward God's bride up to now? Why?

   _____

   _____

   _____

2. What in the text above motivates you to treat the church with love?

   _____

   _____

   _____

3. Suppose the director of children's ministry in your church is a control freak, and she is hard for parents to deal with. You could be one of those parents who must interact with her. How can you be helpful, as opposed to just getting frustrated with her? What is one small step forward that you could take?

   _____

   _____

   _____

4. Identify a hole or a need in your church. How can you be a force for good in that situation, even if you start only by praying lovingly for the people involved and the situation?

Day 3: A Spiritual Father and Spiritual Brothers and Sisters

For by the grace given me I say to every one of you: Do not think of yourself more highly than you ought, but rather think of yourself with sober judgment, in accordance with the faith God has distributed to each of you. For just as each of us has one body with many members, and these members do not all have the same function, so in Christ we, though many, form one body, and each member belongs to all the others. We have different gifts, according to the grace given to each of us. If your gift is prophesying, then prophesy in accordance with your faith; if it is serving, then serve; if it is teaching, then teach; if it is to encourage, then give encouragement; if it is giving, then give generously; if it is to lead, do it diligently; if it is to show mercy, do it cheerfully.

Love must be sincere. Hate what is evil; cling to what is good. Be devoted to one another in love. Honor one another above yourselves. Never be lacking in zeal, but keep your spiritual fervor, serving the Lord. Be joyful in

Many Christians want a spiritual Father but don't want spiritual brothers or sisters or even parents. But God calls us to become a spiritual family.

Consider the picture of maturity in **Romans 12:3–18**. It would be impossible to grow up into these habits without a spiritual family in which we can practice them. We need a family to help us grow up, just as physical babies need families to help them grow up.

As a parent I know that each one of my kids has something they can do to contribute to the family. They have time and hands that can help with the important chores. They have different abilities waiting to be discovered and developed to serve now and in the future in their own families. Not everything done for the family is fun—most would agree that doing the dishes isn't an activity we enjoy but a service we perform.

Often people want to do only what they are passionate about, using a gift they enjoy contributing with. Yet in fact we are servants who sacrifice for the good of others if we are becoming anything like Jesus. Yes, we will enjoy some of the things we do. But many things are an act of giving our life away for others, even when it isn't appreciated. We live with a whole new mind-set of loving others in both words and action (**1 John 3:16–18**).

We aren't just consumers. As the Word tells us, it is more blessed to give than to receive. We all have something to add. We also value what others have to add to us and to the family. We are incomplete without their abilities and perspectives (1 Cor. 12:12–26), and when their perspectives are different from ours, we must remember they are not even our enemies. God longs for us to both contribute and accept the contribution of everyone in the family. Humility is not only to serve but to value other people and their ability to give to us something that is needed. This is how we become complete and mature as a family.

1. What can we learn from Romans 12:3–18 and 1 John 3:16–18 about how believers are to treat each other? Highlight each of the practices listed in those Scriptures. Which of these come easily to you?

_____

_____

_____

_____

2. Which of these practices are challenging for you?

_____

_____

_____

3. Why is each of these practices especially difficult for you?

_____

_____

_____

_____

_____

4. What opportunity do you have to do one of these practices in your spiritual family this week? If you can't identify one on your own, ask someone in your small group to help you.

_____

_____

_____

hope, patient in affliction, faithful in prayer. Share with the Lord's people who are in need. Practice hospitality.

Bless those who persecute you; bless and do not curse. Rejoice with those who rejoice; mourn with those who mourn. Live in harmony with one another. Do not be proud, but be willing to associate with people of low position. Do not be conceited.

Do not repay anyone evil for evil. Be careful to do what is right in the eyes of everyone. If it is possible, as far as it depends on you, live at peace with everyone. (Rom. 12:3–18)

This is how we know what love is: Jesus Christ laid down his life for us. And we ought to lay down our lives for our brothers and sisters. If anyone has material possessions and sees a brother or sister in need but has no pity on them, how can the love of God be in that person? Dear children, let us not love with words or speech but with actions and in truth. (1 John 3:16–18)

Day 4: Spiritual Family Time

Jesus did teach large crowds, and the early church did meet as a large group in the temple courts. But Jesus pushed further and deeper in a small group of twelve men, and the early church followed that example by meeting in smaller groups in homes. Jesus even chose three men (Peter, James, and John) to be His closest friends. He spent a lot of time investing relationally. The apostle Paul also reinforced the relational aspect with those he discipled (**Phil. 4:9**).

Whatever you have learned or received or heard from me, or seen in me—put it into practice. And the God of peace will be with you. (Phil. 4:9)

In the same way, therefore, every Christian needs to be part of these environments:

1. Devotions one-on-one with Jesus.

2. A spiritual friendship with one or two or three people, a circle where it is safe enough to confess sins.

3. A discipleship group of up to about twelve people.

4. Worship as a church body, as well as the work done corporately as we all use our gifts like a team.

God's Word and some measure of relationship are integral to each environment.

Often the only one of these environments a Christian is involved in is the church service, the weekend large group. This will never be enough to help you grow spiritually—you cannot fit all that God knows you need into one hour a week. Hebrews 3:12–13 says we must encourage one another daily so our hearts are not hardened by sin's deceitfulness.

Small groups are the place where we learn to be brothers and sisters in practice. We were created for relationship, but we lost it because of sin. God has given us examples within the church to show us what love looks like. We have a large group where the gift of teaching can give us good information about love, but relationships reinforce what it really looks like in practice. We have Jesus, who is the perfect model in Scripture, and then mature believers, who have been conformed to look like Christ by the power of the Holy Spirit changing them.

We need living models of what love looks like, because the love our physical families passed on to most of us is distorted. Some of us had healthy Christian families, but many of us didn't. One of the church's primary jobs is to show new believers what a family is supposed to look like so that parents can learn to disciple their children in the next generation. Then the Christian family becomes a disciple-making entity that feeds the church, and the home group becomes the place where new believers can see the principles of maturity and family lived out.

Also, real learning happens best in discussion and storytelling and modeling. That's the way Jesus taught His disciples. Sermons are important, but only 20 percent of the population learns best through hearing. I am not saying that they don't learn anything in a large group setting, but what happens in relationship unpacks the teaching in a way that everyone can learn best. They can see it done before their eyes and then are allowed to try it with good coaching.

Again, good teaching is biblical and essential to the life of every believer, but in relationship we unpack proper application—next steps for every believer. So many see the four environments like a smorgasbord where they get to pick whatever they like to put on their spiritual plate. They pile it high with one kind of spiritual food, so to speak, and leave the rest. One person loves worship music and checks out during the rest of the service; another likes a style of preaching and surfs the web if the message is not to their liking. Someone else just likes hanging out with Christians in a small group. This is not what God tells us about a healthy spiritual diet—we need worship and teaching and relationship and service.

This means we will have to change our lifestyle. We will have to put Jesus and His commands first, as the early church did in

They devoted themselves to the apostles' teaching and to fellowship, to the breaking of bread and to prayer. Everyone was filled with awe at the many wonders and signs performed by the apostles. All the believers were together and had everything in common. They sold property and possessions to give to anyone who had need. Every day they continued to meet together in the temple courts. They broke bread in their homes and ate together with glad and sincere hearts. (Acts 2:42–46)

Acts 2:42–46. They embraced teaching, fellowship, and prayer. They met regularly in large group settings and from house to house. They followed the recipe for the faith that Jesus had created, and it led to a life of awe and power that was noticed by others.

1. Look at the four environments that every Christian needs. Which ones are you participating in? Which are missing from your life? How is that affecting you?

   _____

   _____

   _____

2. Are you spending time alone with God each day? If you are, what are the benefits? If you're not, who could help you make that more a part of your life?

   _____

   _____

   _____

3. Who are the one or two people you can trust to know your needs and the things you struggle with? If you don't have such people in your life, how could you go about building a friendship that could go that deep? Who would you *like* to be in close relationship with?

   _____

   _____

   _____

4. If you resist going deep with anybody, why do you think that's the case?

   _____

   _____

   _____

5. What *didn't* you learn about relationships from your family of origin?

   _____

   _____

   _____

Day 5: Spiritual Parenting

A spiritual father or mother is committed to helping the younger believer grow up into maturity, loving God and others well. Spiritual parents give much more than good advice; they are available with a listening ear and practical modeling of how to do healthy relationships.

My own natural birth father and mother became my spiritual parents also. In my teen years, I played the prodigal, and my dad waited and prayed along with my wonderful mom. He would not let me destroy the road home to my mother and him no matter how hard I tried. Once I was restored to Christ, my dad walked me through the stages of spiritual growth. He answered my questions and gave me things to read. He walked me through decisions I had to make. He wisely helped me deal with the consequences caused by my past. He helped me understand the need for connection to the family of God. He and my mom walked me through the pain that relationships even in the body of Christ can cause. He helped me understand I needed to forgive and look past the faults of others.

Later he helped me understand that God had saved me for a purpose and that I wasn't meant to just attend church—I had something to offer the body of Christ. When I finally started to serve and didn't get what I thought I was going to, he helped me understand that I serve Jesus because of what He has done for me, not to gain from men. All along the way, he walked me through to maturity—not just in the church but in my marriage and eventually even helping me negotiate a rebellious child.

So few of us have had good spiritual parents, which is why so few of us have grown to maturity.

In writing to **Titus (2:2–5)**, Paul called on the older women to teach the younger women how to be mature. And Paul's letters to Timothy and Titus show how he was a spiritual parent to these younger men. Timothy knew all about Paul's way of life (**2 Tim.**

Teach the older men to be temperate, worthy of respect, self-controlled, and sound in faith, in love and in endurance.

Likewise, teach the older women to be reverent in the way they live, not to be slanderers or addicted to much wine, but to teach what is good. Then they can urge the younger women to love their husbands and children, to be self-controlled and pure, to be busy at home, to be kind, and to be subject to their husbands, so that no one will malign the word of God. (Titus 2:2–5)

You, however, know all about my teaching, my way of life, my purpose, faith, patience, love, endurance. (2 Tim. 3:10)

You have heard me teach things that have been confirmed by many reliable witnesses. Now teach these truths to other trustworthy people who will be able to pass them on to others. (2 Tim. 2:2 NLT)

3:10). He had traveled with Paul and watched how he operated. Timothy received his gifting and authority when Paul laid hands on him (2 Tim. 1:6). When they were apart, Paul encouraged Timothy through letters, calling him his child in the faith and offering guidance for his ministry. Paul sent Timothy out to serve, but he maintained a close relationship with him. He admonished Timothy to be a spiritual parent to some reliable young men who would eventually be able to do the same for others (**2 Tim. 2:2**).

1. Do you have, or have you had, a spiritual parent? How has that affected your ability to grow mature in loving God and others?

_____

_____

_____

2. Do you want a spiritual parent? Why or why not?

_____

_____

_____

3. What would you like to ask a spiritual parent? What would you like to receive from a spiritual parent?

_____

_____

_____

4. If you don't have a spiritual parent, do you know anyone who is mature enough to serve in that role? If so, who? How could you ask for some of that person's time to help you grow?

_____

_____

_____

5. What are the key insights you have had in Week 4 of this study? What do you want to take from this week and apply to your life?

_____

_____

_____

Growing Together

Day 1: For any who are willing, share your response to question 3. Allow group members who have experienced healing from past hurts to share how that healing came about.

Let members commit once again to make the group a safe, confidential place to share past hurts and present reluctance to trust. Avoid giving advice unless it is requested.

Day 2: Share a life story illustrating how you or someone you know became a force for good in a difficult situation— whether it was a hole that needed mending or a need that had gone unmet in the church.

Day 3: Review your list of practices in question 1 and your response in question 2. Discuss these with your group.

Day 4: Review the four environments at the opening of Day 4. Have a group discussion about them and how each one has benefited your growth or how you might be struggling with one.

Day 5: Share any key insights you have had in Week 4 and what you'd like to apply.

Check in on the accountability requests from Week 1.

Pray for those on Week 1's prayer list.

Week 5

Pride, the Relational Killer

For the rest of this book, we're going to talk about how to have mature relationships. This week we'll explore a crucial character quality: humility. I well know the importance of humility, because as a pastor I was almost derailed by pride.

A few years back, some of my elders asked me to work on an area of my life they believed needed some attention. They felt I wasn't listening to them enough and had fallen into a pattern of seeking to convince rather than listening. When I disagreed with them, they felt like I was cutting them off and not considering their opinions highly enough.

The specific area of disagreement was that I wanted to focus on expanding our church by reaching out to the lost, while they thought we needed a season for those already in the church to be discipled into maturity. I did not take their point of view very well. I was frustrated and didn't want to hear it, so I began to contemplate whether it was time to leave, to begin something new somewhere else. The way I responded to them wasn't in humility but rather in frustration.

But as I talked with my spiritual counselors, they challenged my thinking. Added to this, on a trip to India, I spent time with a leader named K. P. Yohannon. As I shared my thoughts, he asked me to read a book he had written (*Touching Godliness*). The book challenged me in ways that I had not considered before, and it lined up perfectly with what my spiritual counselors in my church were saying, as well as my father and others I had trusted for years.

Several of these counselors had asked me the same question the book addressed (which is usually a sign God is speaking). They asked if I believed God speaks through the leadership team. One man asked, "Do you believe God speaks to you only and then it's your job to tell the team what you think, or is it your job to share what you think God is saying and then to seek confirmation through wise counsel? Do you allow the group to pray about it and then come together to discern God's direction?" In each case they knew the answer, and they knew I knew it because of what I had taught for years, but they wanted me to say it out loud. They asked me to reaffirm that, even for a leader, humility is a characteristic of maturity. They asked if the elders wanted me to do something contrary to the Word or just contrary to my plan.

As I prayed about all of this and let others speak into my life, I knew what I needed to do: submit to the authority of the plurality of elders. As I prayed for help, I began to really try to hear what they were saying. I realized that they had been praying and desired to do what God wanted too.

In the end I accepted the elders' decision to change our emphasis for a season. I also told them that I heard their concerns about my attitude as a leader. I told them I wanted to submit to their authority.

Leadership comes with potential temptations that can lead a person to destruction. It is also a responsibility that comes with accountability. I didn't want to be a dictator. See, God wanted me to *be* something before He wanted me to *do* or *lead* something. God wanted me to be in relationship with Him and these elders. He wanted me to love and be loved, to know and be known.

As we've seen, we were built for relationship, but because of sin, relationship is a real struggle. Yet God has reconciled us to Himself and has given us the ministry of reconciliation. We are becoming peacemakers, lovers of God and lovers of others, especially of those in the family of God. We have the Holy Spirit, who produces peace in us and around us; we have the example of Christ; we have the Word; and we have the example of mature believers to follow. All of these resources can help us grow in humility and short-circuit the enemy's efforts to derail us through pride.

Day 1: Jesus or the Devil

Spiritual maturity is Christlikeness, and love is central to that. The kind of love we're talking about is an act of the will to lay down our lives for another. It's to give others what they need rather than what they deserve. Jesus gave us this model for us to emulate. In order to love like this, we must become humble as Jesus was humble. Humility doesn't mean thinking less of yourself; it means thinking of yourself less. Humility sees others not as tools or possessions but as people whom God loves, and it considers the interests of others over our own.

1. In **Philippians 2:1–4**, what character qualities does Paul urge his readers to cultivate? Highlight them. How is each of them related to humility?

   _____

   _____

   _____

   _____

   _____

   _____

2. According to **Philippians 2:5–8**, how did Jesus set an example of humility?

   _____

   _____

   _____

In humility, Jesus submitted Himself to His Father's authority. He submitted to human authorities to the point of letting them crucify Him. He humbled Himself before His disciples, washing their feet (John 13:1–17). He sought the glory of the Father and the good of others at the expense of Himself.

By contrast, the devil is the ultimate example of pride. He refused to submit to the Father. He became self-absorbed and wanted

Therefore if you have any encouragement from being united with Christ, if any comfort from his love, if any common sharing in the Spirit, if any tenderness and compassion, then make my joy complete by being like-minded, having the same love, being one in spirit and of one mind. Do nothing out of selfish ambition or vain conceit. Rather, in humility value others above yourselves, not looking to your own interests but each of you to the interests of the others. (Phil. 2:1–4)

In your relationships with one another, have the same mindset as Christ Jesus:
Who, being in very nature God,
did not consider equality with
God something to be used to
his own advantage;
rather, he made himself nothing
by taking the very nature of a
servant,
being made in human likeness.
And being found in appearance as
a man,
he humbled himself
by becoming obedient to death—
even death on a cross!
(Phil. 2:5–8)

to put his throne alongside God's. He tries to get us to join him by following our own hearts, trusting only ourselves, living for our own glory, getting others to serve us rather than serving them.

All of you, clothe yourselves with humility toward one another, because,
"God opposes the proud
but shows favor to the humble."
(1 Pet. 5:5)

3. Think about **1 Peter 5:5**. Why do you suppose God opposes the proud?

_____

_____

_____

Such "wisdom" does not come down from heaven but is earthly, unspiritual, demonic. For where you have envy and selfish ambition, there you find disorder and every evil practice.

But the wisdom that comes from heaven is first of all pure; then peace-loving, considerate, submissive, full of mercy and good fruit, impartial and sincere. Peacemakers who sow in peace reap a harvest of righteousness.
(James 3:15–18)

4. In **James 3:15–18**, James contrasts two kinds of wisdom—a false kind and a true kind. How is pride central to demonic "wisdom"? How is humility central to heavenly wisdom?

_____

_____

_____

5. Take a look at your own life. Where do you see signs of self-absorption?

_____

_____

_____

6. How can we tell the difference between healthy self-care and self-absorption? If you don't know, who could help you as a model or as someone to ask?

_____

_____

_____

Day 2: Under God's Authority

For the rest of this week, we're going to look at how pride and humility play out when we relate to authority. Many people like the idea of being saved from hell, but they still want to rule their own lives. Rather than loving God and seeking His heart and His good, they want to use God as a tool for their own glory. They want Jesus as their Savior but not their Lord. This is pride, and it's unacceptable to the Lord Jesus. It is sobering to read the Lord's warning to those who claim to be doing His will but are actually doing their own thing.

1. When **Matthew 7:21–23** speaks of doing the will of the Father in heaven, what specific commands of the Father come to mind for you? What commands have been discussed in this workbook (for example, **Matt. 22:34–40**)?

   _____

   _____

   _____

2. How does it affect you to think of Jesus saying, "I never knew you" to those who disregard these commands? Why?

   _____

   _____

   _____

Other people accept that Jesus is Lord but don't accept His authority as it comes through the authority He gives to people in our lives. For instance, God's Word tells children to obey their parents, wives to submit to their husbands, employees/slaves to submit to their masters, Christians to submit to the elders of their churches, and citizens to submit to the government (Eph. 5:21–6:9; 1 Pet. 5:1–5; Rom. 13:1–7). The exception is when one of these authorities wants to do something that contradicts God's Word.

Not everyone who calls out to me, "Lord! Lord!" will enter the Kingdom of Heaven. Only those who actually do the will of my Father in heaven will enter. On judgment day many will say to me, "Lord! Lord! We prophesied in your name and cast out demons in your name and performed many miracles in your name." But I will reply, "I never knew you. Get away from me, you who break God's laws." (Matt. 7:21–23 NLT)

Hearing that Jesus had silenced the Sadducees, the Pharisees got together. One of them, an expert in the law, tested him with this question: "Teacher, which is the greatest commandment in the Law?"

Jesus replied: "'Love the Lord your God with all your heart and with all your soul and with all your mind.' This is the first and greatest commandment. And the second is like it: 'Love your neighbor as yourself.' All the Law and the Prophets hang on these two commandments." (Matt. 22:34–40)

In each case, God's Word tells the people in authority to treat those under them with love and care, not abusing the authority entrusted to them. Leadership carries a responsibility to lay down your life for the sheep, not a privilege given so that you can use people for your own glory and good. Those of us who have experienced the abuse of authority often react by rejecting all authority, but that is a spiritually immature response driven by pain and fear rather than love for God and others.

Without authority and submission there can be no

- government that works—only anarchy
- homes that have peace and children who are raised to know Jesus
- marriages that work
- businesses that succeed
- discipleship that teaches and shapes
- accountability that changes people
- churches that work together to make disciples
- church discipline that protects the family of God

3. Have you experienced the abuse of authority? How does your experience affect the way you relate to authority figures now?

_____

_____

_____

_____

4. How do you respond to the idea that authority is necessary for families, churches, and societies?

_____

_____

_____

5. On pages 91–92 I talk about my own experience of being a senior pastor and yet heeding the counsel from my elders and other advisers. Would you be more comfortable being

under someone's authority if you knew that this person was humble enough to heed authority in his or her life? Explain.

_____

_____

_____

Day 3: The Lord's Church

And I tell you that you are Peter, and on this rock I will build my church, and the gates of Hades [hell] will not overcome it. (Matt. 16:18)

When I faced the decision of becoming a pastor, I had a hard time. I saw the church as a losing team because churches were not reaching people outside their walls. They were not seeing conversions, and most of the people in churches didn't look to me like mature lovers of God and others. My father told me that God's church is supposed to win. In **Matthew 16:18**, Jesus tells us that the church is God's idea, and the gates of hell will not prevail against it. That is, *God's* church is God's idea, and the gates of hell won't prevail against God's church. He didn't promise that the gates of hell would not defeat a church, just that it wouldn't defeat His church. So what makes a church His church?

First, God gave the church a mission: disciple making, reaching the world with the message.

Second, God gave the church coaches: elders, overseers, pastors, teachers (Eph. 4:11–13; 1 Tim. 3:1–13). When a new church began in the first century, elders were appointed and given authority to lead.

Third, God gave the church players, in sports vernacular. The leaders were to equip God's people—players—for works of service (Eph. 4:12).

Fourth, He described how leaders and players were to behave as a team. "By this everyone will know that you are my disciples, if you love one another" (John 13:35). There was supposed to be order and submission to authority, with each part of the body doing its job (1 Cor. 12:12–27; 14:33).

In 1 and 2 Timothy, we see Paul laying out Timothy's role. He told Timothy to command certain men to do certain things and not to do other things. He told Timothy he had the authority to command these things because Paul the apostle had laid his hands on him. The bottom line was that God gave His church directives and leaders to follow.

1. To what degree are you on board with the church's mission of making disciples?

1	2	3	4	5
not much				completely

What's the evidence in your life?

_____
_____
_____

2. How comfortable are you with following the leaders in your church?

1	2	3	4	5
not much				completely

Why?

_____
_____
_____

3. How good of a job are your leaders doing at equipping church members for service?

1	2	3	4	5
poor				excellent

What's the evidence?

_____
_____
_____

4. How do you need to grow in order to be a more effective and service-oriented member of your church?

_____
_____
_____

5. How could your church grow spiritually in order to more effectively fulfill its mission?

_____

_____

_____

Day 4: Godly Followers and Leaders

A look at our history explains why many American Christians are resistant to leadership.

First, the early church started with strong leadership and submission to leaders. Over time the leadership of the church became corrupt—they stood between God and man rather than teaching people to have a relationship with God. Since the Reformation in the sixteenth century, many Christians have decided that they don't need spiritual leadership in the church. They are correct that all believers are a royal priesthood with direct access to God through Jesus. But they have swung the pendulum from the extreme controlling leadership of the medieval Catholic Church to the extreme rejection of authority of the modern American church. The pendulum would be better placed in the middle.

In America, people think they should have the right to vote out anyone they don't agree with. They can rally a majority and get what they want. If they don't like something, they start a revolution that leads to a church split.

People resist submitting to the authority of their church. They say they are a part of the "Big-C Church" and therefore have an excuse not to work out struggles or submit when they don't understand a decision made by the local church they attend. They use the Big-C Church argument to avoid being under the authority of one church's leaders. They bounce around from church to church, with no real relationships and no willingness to do what the leaders of a church ask them to do. Few serve in the body, though they are asked to. Few give, even though they are taught to. When this happens, the church becomes more theoretical than actual. The truths that the church is to teach and live become just nice ideas that no one actually lives out. There is no church discipline because the people leave if any is imposed. Also, other church members don't submit to the authority of the elders and follow through with the discipline.

To the elders among you, I appeal as a fellow elder and a witness of Christ's sufferings who also will share in the glory to be revealed: Be shepherds of God's flock that is under your care, watching over them—not because you must, but because you are willing, as God wants you to be; not pursuing dishonest gain, but eager to serve; not lording it over those entrusted to you, but being examples to the flock. And when the Chief Shepherd appears, you will receive the crown of glory that will never fade away.

In the same way, you who are younger, submit yourselves to your elders. All of you, clothe yourselves with humility toward one another, because,

"God opposes the proud
but shows favor to the humble."
(1 Pet. 5:1–5)

Have confidence in your leaders and submit to their authority, because they keep watch over you as those who must give an account. Do this so that their work will be a joy, not a burden, for that would be of no benefit to you. (Heb. 13:17)

As I urged you when I went into Macedonia, stay there in Ephesus so that you may command certain people not to teach false doctrines any longer or to devote themselves to myths and endless genealogies. Such things promote controversial speculations rather

Many people rightly expect their leaders to be shepherds. God requires shepherds to feed the sheep and fight off the wolves—we are not to be hirelings and run from the wolf, as Jesus says. We are to chase the strays and bind up the hurting (Ezek. 34). However, I don't think many of the sheep think they have a responsibility to follow the shepherds.

1. Look through the commands in **1 Peter, Hebrews,** and **1 Timothy** that the apostles gave the early church. What did Peter and the writer to the Hebrews expect of church members? What did Paul expect of the people in the church, given what he commanded Timothy to do?

   _____
   _____
   _____
   _____

Our responsibility to those in authority over us, whether parents, bosses, government officials, or church leaders, is summed up as follows:

- Submit to their authority as long as what they say does not contradict God's Word.
- Don't expect leaders to be perfect. Look past their faults; every leader has them.
- Pray for them.
- Be committed to the family we are in.
- If there is a disagreement, approach leaders humbly.
- Be a part of the solution rather than just a consumer.

2. How do you respond to this list of responsibilities? Which items are hard for you? Why?

   _____
   _____
   _____
   _____

After doing a DiscipleShift training with several leaders, I asked them why they hadn't made hard decisions about direction before, even though they knew their church was off course. They said it was because they could get outvoted by the congregation so they would lose their jobs. I asked them what percent of their people were spiritually mature and they told me between 10 and 20 percent. So I made the point that the church could outvote the spiritual parents if they didn't like the direction they chose. I told them that if we applied this method to parenting, then we should never have more than one or maybe two kids, but never three, because the kids could outvote the parents about bedtime or chores. This made no sense.

3. What does this story say about church structures that give every member a vote on what the leadership does and whether they keep their jobs? Do you think there is a problem with such structures? Why or why not?

_____

_____

_____

_____

A godly leader is one who is growing to look like Jesus. Jesus set the agenda for direction, but His purpose was always to obey God and bring glory to Him. It was always to teach the disciples to know God, to protect them and do what was best for them. It was always about love. Ephesians 5:25–27 gives us the picture of Jesus: though He was Lord, He gave Himself up for the church. Leadership is a responsibility, not a privilege to be used for one's own interests.

Jesus commanded Christian leaders not to be like the Gentile kings who lorded it over others but to be servants (**Mark 10:42–45**). He also expected leaders to make hard decisions to follow Him no matter what the culture or church members said. Jesus did not want His leaders to care more about the approval and applause of the people than they cared about the applause of the Lord. He didn't want politicians—He wanted shepherds who led as Jesus

than advancing God's work—which is by faith. The goal of this command is love, which comes from a pure heart and a good conscience and a sincere faith. Some have departed from these and have turned to meaningless talk. They want to be teachers of the law, but they do not know what they are talking about or what they so confidently affirm. (1 Tim. 1:3–7)

I am writing you these instructions so that, if I am delayed, you will know how people ought to conduct themselves in God's household, which is the church of the living God, the pillar and foundation of the truth. (1 Tim. 3:14–15)

Command and teach these things. Don't let anyone look down on you because you are young, but set an example for the believers in speech, in conduct, in love, in faith and in purity. (1 Tim. 4:11–12)

Jesus called them together and said, "You know that those who are regarded as rulers of the Gentiles lord it over them, and their high officials exercise authority over them. Not so with you. Instead, whoever wants to become great among you must be your servant, and whoever wants to be first must be slave of all. For even the Son of Man did not come to be served, but to serve, and to give his life as a ransom for many." (Mark 10:42–45)

had. Leaders should do this for the good of the people, because God's way is always right, always based on love.

Even church discipline is for the good of the person being disciplined. The purpose is always restoration. The desire is to win a brother back, not to put him out.

4. Has your church implemented a process that intentionally helps every member grow to maturity?

_____

_____

_____

5. How much "like Jesus" is enough for you? Are your expectations of your leaders unreasonably high?

_____

_____

_____

Day 5: Environments for a Mature Disciple

There are four environments every Christian should be participating in:

- A personal relationship with God.
- An organized church—God is a God of order, not of disorder, and He has appointed leadership as a need for the church.
- A home, with relationships to family, extended family, or roommates (for single people living alone, this environment looks different).
- The world, with relationships with bosses, employees, colleagues, parents of one's children's friends, etc.

In the book of **Ephesians,** Paul discusses what maturity looks like in all four spheres of life. He starts with a personal relationship with Jesus—we were all by nature objects of God's wrath, but because of God's great love for us we can be saved by grace through faith. We are saved to do the good works which God planned for us to do before time began.

We need to abide in Christ daily—a prayer life and time with God's Word are essential. A personal relationship with Jesus feeds us, because we do not live on physical bread alone but by every word that proceeds from the mouth of God.

All believers need to become disciple-makers who walk with Jesus wherever they go—ready with answers for those who ask about their faith, ready to serve, ready to bring glory to God as an individual.

Mature believers are able to love God and others well. Mature believers are humble enough to be under God's authority and under the authority God has placed in their lives. They are not too proud to accept the authority of a disciple-maker or a pastor.

Like the rest, we were by nature deserving of wrath. But because of his great love for us, God, who is rich in mercy, made us alive with Christ even when we were dead in transgressions— it is by grace you have been saved. . . . For it is by grace you have been saved, through faith—and this is not from yourselves, it is the gift of God—not by works, so that no one can boast. For we are God's handiwork, created in Christ Jesus to do good works, which God prepared in advance for us to do. (Eph. 2:3–5, 8–10)

1. Are you humble enough to be under the spiritual authority God has placed in your life? What's the evidence?

   _____

   _____

   _____

2. If you are leading someone through a discipleship process, what does godly authority look like when you are in authority?

   _____

   _____

   _____

As a prisoner for the Lord, then, I urge you to live a life worthy of the calling you have received. Be completely humble and gentle; be patient, bearing with one another in love. Make every effort to keep the unity of the Spirit through the bond of peace. . . .

Christ himself gave the apostles, the prophets, the evangelists, the pastors and teachers, to equip his people for works of service, so that the body of Christ may be built up until we all reach unity in the faith and in the knowledge of the Son of God and become mature, attaining to the whole measure of the fullness of Christ.

Then we will no longer be infants, tossed back and forth by the waves, and blown here and there by every wind of teaching and by the cunning and craftiness of people in their deceitful scheming. Instead, speaking the truth in love, we will grow to become in every respect the mature body of

The second environment is the church, both relational groups and organized body life. Paul speaks about the church in Ephesians 3–4. He discusses what unifies us, what leadership God has provided, how we work together so that we mature and bring glory to God. In **Ephesians 4**, Paul unpacks how we resolve conflict and bear with each other and encourage one another.

All believers need to be part of a small enough grouping of Christians that they learn how to relate at that level. Just as the early church met in the temple courts and from house to house, so we also need both the large and the small group. In the small group, we do life together.

All believers also need to participate in an organized and elder-led church. (See Matthew 18:15–17; Romans 12:3–7; 1 Corinthians 12:12–31.) The Holy Spirit gives some gifts to the organized church to do what individuals and small groups cannot do.

3. Review **Ephesians 4** in the margin. What do you think are mature ways of relating to others in the church environment? Give two or three examples.

   _____

   _____

   _____

   _____

   _____

4. If you are asked to do something by way of a sermon or in a small group discussion, what is a mature response?

_____

_____

_____

_____

In **Ephesians 5–6**, Paul talks about the home environment: husbands and wives, parents and children. God desires that families become factories that feed disciples into the body of Christ, disciples who know how to make disciples because they have seen it in their home. Husbands and wives disciple one another, and parents disciple their children.

For unmarried people, the picture is a bit different: mature singles focus on loving their friends and spiritual children.

5. What does a mature husband look like? A mature wife? A mature single?

_____

_____

_____

_____

In Ephesians 6, Paul talks about the environment of the world. He speaks of slaves and masters relating to each other, but we can apply his words to employees and bosses at work. We can also think more broadly about the relationships we have in the world, even if we don't have a job with a boss. How do we relate to unbelievers out in the world? How do we demonstrate what it is to be a disciple of Jesus?

6. Read **Ephesians 6:5–9**. How does a mature person relate to a boss? To co-workers? To the coach of your children's sports team?

_____

_____

_____

him who is the head, that is, Christ. (Eph. 4:1–3, 11–15)

Submit to one another out of reverence for Christ.

Wives, submit yourselves to your own husbands as you do to the Lord. For the husband is the head of the wife as Christ is the head of the church, his body, of which he is the Savior. Now as the church submits to Christ, so also wives should submit to their husbands in everything.

Husbands, love your wives, just as Christ loved the church and gave himself up for her to make her holy, cleansing her by the washing with water through the word, and to present her to himself as a radiant church, without stain or wrinkle or any other blemish, but holy and blameless. In this same way, husbands ought to love their wives as their own bodies. He who loves his wife loves himself. After all, no one ever hated their own body, but they feed and care for their body, just as Christ does the church—for we are members of his body. "For this reason a man will leave his father and mother and be united to his wife, and the two will become one flesh." This is a profound mystery—but I am talking about Christ and the church. However, each one of you also must love his wife as he loves himself, and the wife must respect her husband.

Children, obey your parents in the Lord, for this is right. "Honor your father and mother"—which is the first commandment with a promise—"so that it may go well with you and that you may enjoy long life on the earth."

Fathers, do not exasperate your children; instead, bring them up in the training and instruction of the Lord. (Eph. 5:21—6:4)

Slaves, obey your earthly masters with respect and fear, and with sincerity of heart, just as you would obey Christ. Obey them not only to win their favor when their eye is on you, but as slaves of Christ, doing the will of God from your heart. Serve wholeheartedly, as if you were serving the Lord, not people, because you know that the Lord will reward each one for whatever good they do, whether they are slave or free.

And masters, treat your slaves in the same way. Do not threaten them, since you know that he who is both their Master and yours is in heaven, and there is no favoritism with him. (Eph. 6:5—9)

7. How does a mature believer relate to the government? To the police?

_____

_____

_____

_____

8. What are the key insights you have had in Week 5 of this study? What do you want to take from this week and apply to your life?

_____

_____

_____

_____

Growing Together

Day 1: Question 6 will be especially important to discuss. Think of specific examples that would help illustrate each. Don't be embarrassed if you have trouble telling the difference between self-care and self-absorption. Be where you are, and try to identify what it would be like to have a more mature view of this.

Day 2: Discuss question 3, but avoid turning the meeting into a gripe session about authority, unless your leader feels that doing so will help you clear the air and move forward.

Day 3: Share your answers to question 5. Once again, avoid descending into a gripe session. For those who aren't mature, it can be easier to see a leader's weaknesses than their own. Instead, try to find their strengths and discuss constructive ways you can contribute to making your church better. Any legitimate concerns about leadership are best discussed in private with your group leader or someone they recommend.

Day 4: Now it's the layperson's turn to look at their responsibilities toward leadership. The opening sentence in Day 4 reads, "A look at our history explains why many American Christians are resistant to leadership." What are the ramifications of this in your life and what you might see in your church? Then share your responses to question 2.

Day 5: Discuss the responses of a mature believer to the various entities mentioned in questions 6 and 7. Share some key insights from the week.

Check in on the accountability requests from Week 1.

Pray for those on Week 1's prayer list.

Week 6

Disputable Matters

Years ago when we started Real Life we wanted to be different. We knew few churches were growing with new converts, and the lives of Christians didn't look much different from those of the world. Many of the churches that were growing were being filled up with those who had been to other churches before—just a reshuffling of the same fifty-two cards, so to speak. Also, many churches were splitting for one reason or another, and disgruntled people were moving from church to church rather than experiencing deep-rooted, long-lasting spiritual relationships.

I knew this was a discipleship problem that was keeping people from spiritual maturity as well as affecting the reputation of Jesus with outsiders. I had been one of those people who heard about the Prince of Peace from Christians, I had heard about the Holy Spirit who supposedly creates peace, but then I experienced constant battles and wondered why I would want Him if He didn't even work for Christians.

As I researched the top reasons churches battled internally, I quickly recognized some of the same old subjects: music style, once saved always saved, speaking in tongues, end-times theology, and on the list went. Though differences in theology were often the communicated culprit, I knew that beneath these battles lay personality and relational issues.

In order to be a winning team we had to have unity. Using the sports analogy, it doesn't matter how much talent you have; you can't win if players won't play as a team and work together for the same goal using a shared game plan. Jesus was much more succinct: He said a house divided against itself cannot stand (Mark 3:25). At the same time, the devil was a great divider. He had a habit of bringing attention to differences, not so that people could work things out but so that they would get distracted and spend their energy internally rather than on the mission to reach the world.

I also understood that there was truth in every one of these potentially divisive subjects, and great people who had given their whole lives to Jesus did not see eye to eye on many of them. Now, sincerity is no excuse for false teaching, but these men and women were very committed to the Word of God. What might have been construed as false teaching to some was many times another person reading the Scriptures differently on a subject (not on the bedrock principles of our faith). In other words, these were *disputable* matters. As I studied, I started to ask myself a few questions:

- What does Scripture tell us about what binds us together?
- What does the Bible say, and how was it lived out in the early church?
- What do we do with issues that are disputable, according to Scripture?
- Who decides for the body on disputable issues?
- How are we to act even in the midst of disagreements?

Day 1: Unity and Relationship

Our unity and relationship prove there is something about us that is different from unbelievers. Consider **John 13:35**. Paul tells us what unifies us. Consider what he says in **1 Corinthians 1:10** and **Ephesians 4:1–6**.

1. What unifies us, according to 1 Corinthians 1:10 and Ephesians 4:1–6?

   _____

   _____

   _____

2. Why does this matter?

   _____

   _____

   _____

By calling the church a "body," Paul implies order, authority, and service to one another and to the purpose of the mind that directs the body. Christ is the head, the brain, the authority that directs by the power of the Holy Spirit the actions of the body as each part does its work.

   We have one Holy Spirit indwelling all of us and producing the fruit of the Spirit in us. The inspiration of the Holy Spirit gives us Scripture about truth and right behavior.

   We have one hope: heaven, Jesus's second coming, the new heavens and new earth.

   We have one Lord: Jesus, the King of His kingdom.

   We have one faith: that we are saved by grace through faith to do the good works that God planned for us to do before time began. Our faith includes behavior that is in line with the gospel.

By this everyone will know that you are my disciples, if you love one another. (John 13:35)

I appeal to you, dear brothers and sisters, by the authority of our Lord Jesus Christ, to live in harmony with each other. Let there be no divisions in the church. Rather, be of one mind, united in thought and purpose. (1 Cor. 1:10 NLT)

Therefore I, a prisoner for serving the Lord, beg you to lead a life worthy of your calling, for you have been called by God. Always be humble and gentle. Be patient with each other, making allowance for each other's faults because of your love. Make every effort to keep yourselves united in the Spirit, binding yourselves together with peace. For there is one body and one Spirit, just as you have been called to one glorious hope for the future. There is one Lord, one faith, one baptism, one God and Father of all, who is over all, in all, and living through all. (Eph. 4:1–6 NLT)

We have one baptism: one outward sign and public confession of becoming a Christian.

We have one God: the Trinity, who is Father, Son, and Holy Spirit.

As time went on in the church, people began to ask questions about details. For instance, Scripture makes it clear that Jesus had human flesh and was like us in all ways but also that He was God in the flesh. People wanted to know how this could be, so they dove into the details. They disagreed, and rather than just accepting the simple truth, they divided on their various explanations of an eternal truth that could not be understood through human wisdom.

This still happens. Rather than keeping things simple, accepting what God's Word says and moving toward working together to bless others, we sit around and come up with ways to fight with one another.

In football we knew if we could get the other team fighting in the huddle, we had them at the line of scrimmage. The devil knows this too, and he has caused us to deny truth because we can't understand it or to make truth more complex and add to it.

3. In your experience, what do Christians fight over? Make a list of topics you have heard them fight over.

   _____

   _____

   _____

   _____

4. What do you think mature believers should do if they disagree? How do they handle disagreement if they are mature in loving God and loving others?

   _____

   _____

   _____

   _____

Day 2: When Cultures Collide

The New Testament shows us how to handle differences because the first generation of believers had a collision of two very different cultures.

The first was Jewish. Jesus and all of His disciples were Jews, and they lived according to the Old Testament law. The law had a purpose: to reveal what sin is and to reveal the cost—blood and death. The Old Testament also revealed that God was merciful enough to accept a sacrifice in our stead if we truly had a change of mind that led to a change of action (repentance). The Old Testament system was in a sense a prophecy fulfilled in Jesus's life, death, and resurrection. Having served its purpose, the Old Testament system of temple sacrifices became obsolete after Jesus's resurrection. But it took some time for Jesus's disciples to realize this, because they had spent their whole lives living under the Jewish system. They assumed that Jewish practices, such as circumcision and the kosher food laws, would continue.

The second culture was Gentile. The Gentiles worshiped numerous false gods by offering animal sacrifices to them. They also worshiped fertility gods and goddesses through sexual rites. They weren't accustomed to avoiding work on one day a week (the Sabbath, which Jews kept). And circumcision horrified them; they thought it mutilated the body. When Gentiles became Christian, it wasn't immediately clear to everyone which of their familiar practices they would have to give up and which Jewish customs they would have to adopt. There was considerable disagreement about this.

The apostle Paul thought deeply about these disagreements. By the power of the Holy Spirit, he was led to write down principles that are always right for all Christians everywhere in every generation, whether Jewish or Gentile (**Rom. 14**). Love was always right, for instance. He also proposed that some behaviors were always

Accept the one whose faith is weak, without quarreling over disputable

matters. One person's faith allows them to eat anything, but another, whose faith is weak, eats only vegetables. The one who eats everything must not treat with contempt the one who does not, and the one who does not eat everything must not judge the one who does, for God has accepted them. Who are you to judge someone else's servant? To their own master, servants stand or fall. And they will stand, for the Lord is able to make them stand.

One person considers one day more sacred than another; another considers every day alike. Each of them should be fully convinced in their own mind. Whoever regards one day as special does so to the Lord. Whoever eats meat does so to the Lord, for they give thanks to God; and whoever abstains does so to the Lord and gives thanks to God. For none of us lives for ourselves alone, and none of us dies for ourselves alone. If we live, we live for the Lord; and if we die, we die for the Lord. So, whether we live or die, we belong to the Lord. For this very reason, Christ died and returned to life so that he might be the Lord of both the dead and the living.

You, then, why do you judge your brother or sister? Or why do you treat them with contempt? For we will all stand before God's judgment seat. . . .

Therefore let us stop passing judgment on one another. Instead, make

wrong for all Christians everywhere. Sex with a temple prostitute, for instance, was always wrong. And then there were what he called disputable matters, things about which mature Christians could differ and yet still love one another and remain in fellowship.

Paul recognized that, based on their upbringing, some people would be bothered by some behaviors that others were not bothered by. Rather than list a truth about every situation, he gave us some general principles that govern the way we deal with others. Paul saw that not every truth is equally important. We recognize this truth every day in the world we live in. Some things are right or wrong, and some are just preferential. In part, wisdom is to know the difference. The color of my house is not as important as gravity. I can make a poor decision about the color and still be fine, but if I choose not to accept the truth of gravity, I could die. The truth that God is a Trinity, three equal Persons in one undivided God, is essential Christian truth. We may not understand it, but it is bedrock truth. But whether or not we should eat meat is something we as Jesus-followers can disagree about and still remain united under the lordship of Jesus Christ.

Ignorance and error about some things are inevitable because we are all fallible. So it's very important that we don't confuse essential truths with disputable matters.

1. From the above text, including the Scripture in Romans 14, what were some of the things Jewish Christians and Gentile Christians probably disagreed about?

   _____
   _____
   _____
   _____
   _____

2. Why is the category of disputable matters important to keep in mind?

   _____
   _____
   _____

3. How would you go about deciding whether something is a disputable matter about which mature Christians can disagree?

_____

_____

_____

4. What can we learn from Paul's statement in Romans 14 regarding making decisions about things that prick our consciences?

_____

_____

_____

5. If you want to do some further study, read through 1 Corinthians and list all of the things Paul knew the early church was arguing about. Then list the things Paul gave them permission to disagree over.

_____

_____

_____

_____

_____

_____

6. What are some of the disputable matters Christians wrestle with today? How could thinking of them as disputable matters help Christians live together in love despite these differences?

_____

_____

_____

_____

_____

up your mind not to put any stumbling block or obstacle in the way of a brother or sister. I am convinced, being fully persuaded in the Lord Jesus, that nothing is unclean in itself. But if anyone regards something as unclean, then for that person it is unclean. If your brother or sister is distressed because of what you eat, you are no longer acting in love. Do not by your eating destroy someone for whom Christ died. (Rom. 14:1–10, 13–15)

Day 3: Food Sacrificed to Idols

Now about food sacrificed to idols: We know that "We all possess knowledge." But knowledge puffs up while love builds up. Those who think they know something do not yet know as they ought to know. But whoever loves God is known by God.

So then, about eating food sacrificed to idols: We know that "An idol is nothing at all in the world" and that "There is no God but one." For even if there are so-called gods, whether in heaven or on earth (as indeed there are many "gods" and many "lords"), yet for us there is but one God, the Father, from whom all things came and for whom we live; and there is but one Lord, Jesus Christ, through whom all things came and through whom we live.

But not everyone possesses this knowledge. Some people are still so accustomed to idols that when they eat sacrificial food they think of it as having been sacrificed to a god, and since their conscience is weak, it is defiled. But food does not bring us near to God; we are no worse if we do not eat, and no better if we do.

Be careful, however, that the exercise of your rights does not become a stumbling block to the weak. For if

In **1 Corinthians 8**–10, Paul has a long discussion about something that was a disputable matter among Christians of his day. The question was whether Christians were permitted to eat meat sacrificed to idols. At that time, most of the butchers in a typical town were attached to pagan temples. They got their meat from the temple sacrifices. Also, many business meetings for upper-class men were held at temples and served meat from the sacrifices. Often the only place to get meat that wasn't sacrificed to idols was at a Jewish butcher, who would sometimes be unwilling to sell to Christians.

Some Christians believed that the idols worshiped in pagan temples were nothing, so eating the meat was fine. Others believed the idols were demons, so eating the meat was abhorrent. The latter group argued that it was better to be vegetarian than to have anything to do with pagan sacrifices. This dispute became an issue of unity; it seemed important enough to fight and even divide over.

Paul's discussion of this quarrel isn't black and white. On the one hand, he says, the idols are indeed nothing, so eating the meat doesn't pollute the eater. People are saved by grace through faith, and eating meat doesn't affect their standing before God. Their faith saves them when they thank the real God for the food.

On the other hand, Paul says, if you come from a pagan background of worshiping idols, and your conscience bothers you when you eat the meat, then don't do it. It would be better to be vegetarian than to do something that doesn't seem right to you.

Second, if a young believer comes from a pagan background and is confused when he sees you eat the sacrificed meat, then the loving thing to do might be to skip the meat at that time and help your young friend make his clean break from idolatry. You may have the right to do something, but it is sometimes more loving to lay down your rights for the good of another person. You may eat meat in private but not in front of this vulnerable person.

Third, Paul says, while your conscience is a good guide, it may mislead you. So do a careful study in Scripture and make sure you get wise counsel from mature believers in your spiritual family about the decision you face. Before you make a final decision, be curious rather than judgmental about why other believers may be allowing or not allowing something.

And finally, when you come to a decision about what is right for you regarding a disputable matter, don't demand that all Christians agree with you. Some things are always right, and some are always wrong, but there are a number of disputable matters on which faithful Christians will disagree. Christians are God's servants, and it's not our business to pass judgment on someone else's servant. God will be the judge. Remember that Paul also told the Christians to bear with one another's faults, so keep your own opinion to yourself on these matters.

Paul's teaching applies today in many areas. For example, you may not have a problem playing cards, but if your brother has a gambling addiction, you are not loving your brother by inviting him to join you in a card game. For you, cards are nothing, but for him they may trigger a destructive habit.

If you have relationship with those around you and you desire that they know Jesus in a deeper way, then you are careful about what you do because you love Jesus and them. There are so many things that Christians can fight about: being Republican or Democrat, drinking alcohol, gambling, spanking, movies, and so on. As believers we seek to know the people around us and do what is best for them.

I love hunting and fishing, but in our church we have some who see killing animals for sport as evil. With them I don't talk about it. I don't allow their hatred for killing and eating a deer to keep me from hunting, but I am also sensitive to their conscience and feelings, so I keep it to myself around them. I won't allow them to convince me that it's wrong, and if they want to lovingly talk about our difference of opinion scripturally, I will try to discuss my convictions on the situation, but I will not try to force a secondary issue down their throat. I will not tell them they have to hunt or eat

someone with a weak conscience sees you, with all your knowledge, eating in an idol's temple, won't that person be emboldened to eat what is sacrificed to idols? So this weak brother or sister, for whom Christ died, is destroyed by your knowledge. When you sin against them in this way and wound their weak conscience, you sin against Christ. Therefore, if what I eat causes my brother or sister to fall into sin, I will never eat meat again, so that I will not cause them to fall. (1 Cor. 8:1–13)

119

meat to be a believer. Our common faith makes us both saved, but the issue is disputable, and I will be sensitive to it. We can agree to disagree on the issue and move on together because we share faith in the most important things. Again, Paul's answer is not to divide into the meat-eating church and the vegetarian church or the church that follows Paul and the church that follows Apollos—or the speaking-in-tongues church and the non-speaking-in-tongues church. When there is a problem, it brings God glory when people do the opposite (unite) of what the world does (divide). Just as marriage is meant to be forever (with rare and extreme reasons to separate), so the family of God is meant to be for life.

1. Why did some believers in Paul's day think eating meat sacrificed to idols was fine? Why did others believe it was terrible?

   _____

   _____

   _____

2. Under what circumstances did Paul say it was fine to eat this meat? Under what circumstances did he recommend that a person not eat the meat?

   _____

   _____

   _____

3. Apply the case of eating meat offered to idols to two modern situations: playing cards and hunting. In what other modern situations could this precept be applied? How would you apply it? (When you meet with your group to discuss this question, be alert to areas where you disagree with other members. Don't assume that everyone in the group sees a disputable matter in the same way.)

   _____

   _____

   _____

   _____

   _____

   _____

4. What for you are the most helpful aspects of the discernment process outlined here?

Day 4: Dealing with Conflict

Conflicts will arise in every church because we have different views on disputable matters. We have different personalities, filters, giftings, and so on. We also have a spiritual enemy who will seek to cause misunderstanding so that he can divide us. The only way broken people can be in relationship is if grace giving is a constant part of doing life as a believer. Love keeps no record of wrongs.

God's Word tells us that we cannot let a bitter root grow up in us until it defiles us and others (**Heb. 12:15**). It also tells us to bear with one another's faults. Though we would love to grow up into perfection and have no faults, that is not possible this side of heaven. We would like people to remember that we will make mistakes no matter how hard we try. We need understanding and forgiveness. At the same time we must remember this about others as well. With this in mind:

- Have right expectations. Expect others to have faults. Bear with them. Don't be easily offended.
- Cultivate humility. You have planks in your own eye (**Matt. 7:3–5**). Remember that and work on yourself first. When you do this, it changes your heart from judgment to a desire to help another grow. And in some cases your heart decides to just bear with others instead of pointing out their wrongs.
- Use words that build up rather than offend others (**Eph. 4:29**).
- Be honest with one another when you are hurt. Tell each other the truth quickly. Don't let the sun go down on your anger.
- Choose to love even when you don't feel like it. Love forgives.
- Pray for your brother. Your broken relationships with others do affect how the Lord hears your prayers. For example, husbands: deal with your wife in an understanding way or your prayers are hindered (**1 Pet. 3:7**).

See to it that no one falls short of the grace of God and that no bitter root grows up to cause trouble and defile many. (Heb. 12:15)

Why do you look at the speck of saw-dust in your brother's eye and pay no attention to the plank in your own eye? How can you say to your brother, "Let me take the speck out of your eye," when all the time there is a plank in your own eye? You hypocrite, first take the plank out of your own eye, and then you will see clearly to remove the speck from your brother's eye. (Matt. 7:3–5)

Do not let any unwholesome talk come out of your mouths, but only what is

122

• If your brother has sinned against you, then be honest and confront in love and humility. If the situation is not reconciled, then bring an impartial and mature brother or sister with you to take the next step (**Matt. 18:15–17**). The purpose of Matthew 18 is not to throw the bum out but to restore relationship. God wants problems in the family of God to be dealt with in the family of God. See what Paul says about dealing with lawsuits among believers in 1 Corinthians 6.

With the empowering help of the Holy Spirit, we as Christ-followers are to be courageous. We don't gossip. We don't avoid conflict and allow bitterness to grow up in us. We are peacemakers, which means when we see a lack of peace, we address it rather than allow it. When there is a problem, we follow the principle in Matthew 18, going first to the person privately to try to resolve it. (This takes courage and humility.) We avoid spreading rumors or involving those who aren't part of the problem, because we understand the tongue is a restless evil and can start a fire that disappoints God and ruins His reputation with outsiders. When we have offended someone and they confront us about it, we don't get defensive and we thank them for coming to us. Even if we don't agree with them, we can at least respect that they came to us to work it out.

helpful for building others up according to their needs, that it may benefit those who listen. (Eph. 4:29)

Husbands, in the same way be considerate as you live with your wives, and treat them with respect as the weaker partner and as heirs with you of the gracious gift of life, so that nothing will hinder your prayers. (1 Pet. 3:7)

If your brother or sister sins, go and point out their fault, just between the two of you. If they listen to you, you have won them over. But if they will not listen, take one or two others along, so that every matter may be established by the testimony of two or three witnesses. If they still refuse to listen, tell it to the church; and if they refuse to listen even to the church, treat them as you would a pagan or a tax collector. (Matt. 18:15–17)

1. Think of a conflict you have had that did not go well. How did you or the other person violate one of the principles listed above? (If you discuss these situations in your group, avoid naming names and gossiping.)

   _____

   _____

   _____

2. Think of a conflict you have had that did go well. Which of the above principles did you practice?

   _____

   _____

   _____

3. Are you in the midst of any conflict that is not yet resolved? How do the above principles apply?

_____

_____

_____

4. By temperament, do you prefer to avoid conflict or do you get aggressive in conflict? What would you say are your weak areas when it comes to resolving conflict in a loving and effective way?

_____

_____

_____

_____

5. What questions do you have about conflict resolution that your group might be able to help you with?

_____

_____

_____

_____

Day 5: If All Else Fails

Part of dealing with conflict or discerning God's will in a given situation is to seek wise counsel. More than that, God has given us leaders in the church to help us understand God's will.

Biblical authority is given to the elders to make the final judgment in a disagreement. **Acts 15** recounts the case of a dispute that ended with the apostles and elders making the final call, and it was accepted as God's will.

Yet many Christians do not see themselves as being under the authority of the eldership in a church. They take their me-and-Jesus mentality to the point where, if they disagree with the direction of the church, even on disputable matters, they leave. Leaving a church is appropriate if the leaders are teaching false things about salvation or other core truths of the gospel, but leaving isn't appropriate if the issue is preference about something secondary. Hebrews 13:17 says, "Have confidence in your leaders and submit to their authority, because they keep watch over you as those who must give an account." **First Peter 5:5** tells younger believers to submit to elders. In **Acts 20**, Paul speaks to those he calls "overseers" and says they are shepherds meant to protect the flock. Titus 1:7 says an overseer manages God's household.

To trust the eldership is to bring them into a dispute when all else has failed and to trust their teaching and leadership about what issues are disputable matters. We trust them, knowing that they must give an account to the Lord about their leadership.

For example, every year we have a harvest festival in our church. Some of our people don't want to be involved because they think it is celebrating Halloween. But that's not the reason our leaders do the event. Thousands of people come and have a fun interaction with our church, and it builds a bridge to future interaction. As leaders, we don't ask the people who are bothered by a harvest event to be involved, but we do ask

This brought Paul and Barnabas into sharp dispute and debate with them. So Paul and Barnabas were appointed, along with some other believers, to go up to Jerusalem to see the apostles and elders about this question. (Acts 15:2)

In the same way, you who are younger, submit yourselves to your elders. All of you, clothe yourselves with humility toward one another, because,

> *"God opposes the proud*
>   *but shows favor to the humble."*
> *(1 Pet. 5:5)*

Keep watch over yourselves and all the flock of which the Holy Spirit has made you overseers. Be shepherds of the church of God, which he bought with his own blood. I know that after I leave, savage wolves will come in among you and will not spare the flock. Even from your own number men will arise and distort the truth in order to draw away disciples after them. So be on your guard! Remember that for three years I never stopped warning each of you night and day with tears. (Acts 20:28–31)

them not to judge those who are involved. We ask them to see this as a disputable matter. To trust the leaders is to allow them to make the final decision. Our people trust that authority has been given to us to have the final say in directing the church. And we leaders are responsible to be sensitive to the consciences of some of our flock.

When you have difficult personal decisions to make, you need to be able to trust the disciple-makers in your life as well as the leaders in your church to go to them for counsel as part of the way you discern God's will.

For example, one of our men came to tell me he needed some counsel about going to another church to help them start a home group system. He was a volunteer home group leader and his brother was a pastor of a church across town. After reading one of my books, the pastor was convicted that they were not making disciples, so he asked his brother to come to his church to help him. As a member of our church and under the spiritual authority of our leaders, this man came to ask what he should do. After we prayed about it together, we agreed that it would be good for him to go and help that church.

God's elders are not dictators; they manage God's household with specific, designated authority from the Lord. In some churches, elders exceed their God-assigned responsibilities and demand submission to their decisions on whom a person should marry, what job a person should take, and so on. But the opposite is true in many cases: elders do much less managing and shepherding than what God has intended. It is vital for both leadership and laity to seek strong spiritual relationships and grow into mature disciple-makers. In turn, that type of church will raise up healthy elders who submit to God's instruction on their responsibilities. Those who are a part of the family of God at that place trust them for wise counsel.

For those Christians who say they are part of the church universal and therefore don't need to be committed to a local body and submitted to its leadership, they are sorely mistaken and will almost inevitably suffer for it.

1. Can you imagine going to the leaders of your church to help you work out a dispute with someone else? Why or why not?

2. Can you imagine going to the leaders of your church for wise counsel on what to do in a confusing situation? Why or why not?

3. What is wrong with a me-and-Jesus mentality when it comes to seeking God's will for your life?

4. What would happen in your church if an issue like the harvest festival came up? How would it be handled? How effective do you think your church's approach would be?

5. How do you think leaders can build the kind of trust in their people that is needed to help solve conflicts?

6. What are the key insights you have had in Week 6 of this study? What do you want to take from this week and apply to your life?

Growing Together

Day 1: Question 4 may have been hard to answer. Discuss how disagreements can be handled without leading to broken relationships.

Day 2: In your group, you don't need to solve the problem of any specific disputable matter. Instead, talk about a method for dealing with disputable matters as individuals and as a church body.

Day 3: Review your answer to question 3 and discuss some of these situations in your group. Because some may have strong convictions that vary, be careful to express your own convictions and your opinions of others' with respect and deference. If the discussion becomes heated, let's agree to disagree and move to discussion of question 4.

Day 4: From question 5, discuss any questions you have about conflict resolution. Personal examples can be useful to clarify an issue, but be careful not to divulge names and information that would damage another person's reputation.

Day 5: Look for an honest yet respectful way to talk about how you relate to your leaders and their decisions. Discuss question 4. It will be helpful to learn if your view of your church lines up with the way others in your group see your church. If you see flaws in the way you think your church handles conflict, discuss how you can be part of the solution. (Again, any gripes should be handled privately with your group leader.) Share key insights from the week.

Check in on the accountability requests from Week 1.

Pray for those on Week 1's prayer list.

Week 7

A Better Return for Your Labor

At Real Life Ministries, we regularly hold seminars for pastors and church leaders to train them in our discipleship processes and methodology. Many pastors bring their church staff and key volunteer leadership to go through the two-day experience. During these seminars, we intentionally keep the large-group teaching to a minimum so people can experience discipleship in and through relationship in groups. The groups are led by a combination of our staff and volunteers. We do this because we want the attending pastors to see that relational discipleship in small groups produces an ever-increasing number of leaders—disciples making other disciples. We role-play the discipling process with volunteers in front of the visiting pastors and their staff so they can see how it is done. About thirty RLM volunteers put together the meals and deal with the details in every facet of our time together.

It takes time and hard work to build a team of leaders and volunteers who work well together and genuinely love each other. We aren't just lucky to have the people we do; we have invested deeply in the people whom the Lord has sent to us. We do this because we genuinely believe that teams of mature and maturing people bear much more fruit than individuals working alone. This week you'll have a chance to look at what the Scriptures say about working and growing together as a team and see why it's so beneficial.

Day 1: The Value of Teamwork

Ecclesiastes 4:8–12 paints a picture of a man doing his best to work alone. He's without family or friends, and all he does is work, work, work. He's apparently got plenty to do, and one result of all his hard work is that he's grown wealthy. But his work lacks meaning and he's unhappy. He's unclear about why he is working so hard—he's got no one to share his wealth with.

This was written more than three thousand years ago, but it accurately describes the modern American man who's trying to make it to the top. He's made some poor choices along the way that have left him alone. In the end, he's miserable and depressed. He might own the amazing house and the expensive car, but there is no one in the house or car with him who really knows him at a deep and fulfilling level. He's certainly not satisfied.

This passage reflects many of today's Christians and even our leaders. Some have no problem serving others, but let someone into their heart? No thank you. Yes, we are to serve people, but we also serve *with* them. This gets the work done better, and a work is also done in our own hearts too. When we serve, we are being poured out, but God's plan was to continually pour into us so there is always something to pour out of us. God works through others in our lives, and through His people He pours into us what we need to live and serve. Those who attempt to serve alone, even for a good cause, eventually burn out or develop a calloused and bitter heart, and the greater work of discipling those who can disciple others is thwarted.

This can happen both to single and married people. In fact, mature singles who have invested in deep friendships and have done the hard work of letting themselves be known are more satisfied than married people who don't know how to be intimate with a spouse or close to a friend.

Some Christians see other people as obstacles to getting more done. They think they do their best work when left to themselves.

There was a man all alone;
*   he had neither son nor brother.*
There was no end to his toil,
*   yet his eyes were not content with*
*   his wealth.*
"For whom am I toiling," he asked,
*   "and why am I depriving myself of*
*   enjoyment?"*
This too is meaningless—
*   a miserable business!*

Two are better than one,
*   because they have a good return for*
*   their labor:*
If either of them falls down,
*   one can help the other up.*
But pity anyone who falls
*   and has no one to help them up.*
Also, if two lie down together, they
*   will keep warm.*
*   But how can one keep warm alone?*
Though one may be overpowered,
*   two can defend themselves.*
A cord of three strands is not quickly
*   broken. (Eccles. 4:8–12)*

In my experience, though, the opposite is true. Scripture says the same. If we can see the value of others' differing gifts and perspectives, we can take advantage of these differences in order to succeed in the mission God has given us. For example, in a couple where the husband is the driver and the wife is the nurturer, both attributes are needed for a healthy family.

In **Philippians 1:27**, Paul admonishes us to work together as one. What we most need if we want to be effective as a team is a shared vision and pathway to the goal. A Christ-centered, Holy Spirit–filled team will be led to see more together than they can alone. There may be struggle and disagreement in the process of getting there, but if the team is willing to put in the work, a shared vision ultimately emerges that will create an effective team.

Stand firm in the one Spirit, striving together as one for the faith of the gospel. (Phil. 1:27)

1. What advantages of teamwork does Ecclesiastes 4:8–12 offer?

2. What activities in your day are solitary? What activities are done with a team (even if the whole team isn't in the room together)? What is your response to the idea of making more of your life a team sport?

3. How can you build into your work the advantages of teamwork, even if it's a small step like asking someone to pray for your work and opening up to them about your areas of need?

4. Do you have a shared vision with someone (your spouse, co-workers, friends at church)? If so, what is the vision? If not, what could you do to move toward a shared vision with someone or some group?

5. What are the obstacles to a shared vision? How can they be overcome?

Day 2: Wise Counsel

Some years ago sermon preparation was eating up all my time. I spent between twenty and thirty hours each week just on sermon prep and, quite honestly, still missed the mark. That was on top of the thirty to forty or so other hours I spent in other church-related work. I was running myself ragged, and it was affecting my marriage, my parenting, and my ability to be a good spiritual leader.

I talked to an older pastor about what to do. He had planted a church many years before, and he told me about something he designed in his church called the "Sermon Club." He brought in a bunch of staff members and laypeople for a meeting early in the week to collaborate on the sermon. It was a way to get outside his own perspective.

So I tried it. As I began to do this, I found that in one hour I was getting about fifteen hours' worth of work done. I was able to try out some of my thoughts and ideas on a group who could tell me what they heard. They gave me input that I had not thought about and helped me apply principles. The women in the group helped me see from their perspective and find better ways to relate to women. Younger staff helped me find a way to bridge the teaching to their ministry and gave me better illustrations that could touch the hearts of the young. My older, wiser staff gave me input into how the Greek or Hebrew might be used and offered a more expanded interpretation of Scripture by adding passages to my incomplete view. Our volunteers who attended gave me some thoughts about how the message would apply to the business owner or the employee of a bank and so on.

Sermon Club gave me a faster way to study and a better way to relate to others. By working as a team, I was getting wise counsel and a broader perspective than my own. This freed up time for me to do all that I needed to do as a leader and to be balanced at home.

I discovered other benefits as well. My staff saw that if I could work with others, so could they. If I could seek wise counsel, so could they. It also helped them start to understand how to develop lessons, and this accelerated their growth process in communicating. We developed speakers even as we developed sermons.

Sermon Club is just one example of what **Proverbs 11:14** and **15:22** tell us, that plans succeed with many advisers. Each of us sees only based on our own perspective. Our solutions are limited to what we can discern or have experienced. Individually, we can tend to overcomplicate or oversimplify problems. By working together, though, we get a better view of both problems and solutions. Also, we get far more buy-in if we ask people to participate rather than dictating our understanding of a problem and expecting others to live out our solution.

Pride is what tells us that we understand the problem and have the solution without input from others. Pride says that God tells us directly all we need to know in our me-and-Jesus relationship with God. However, He is the one who tells us that He speaks in and through others in our lives. If He wanted us to only pray and read Scripture, then He would have defined disciple making as simply printing and distributing Bibles. Rather, He said, "Go and make disciples, . . . teaching them to obey everything I have commanded you" (Matt. 28:19–20), learning from godly teachers and wiser, more experienced believers.

For lack of guidance a nation falls,
but victory is won through many advisers. . . .
Plans fail for lack of counsel,
but with many advisers they succeed. (Prov. 11:14; 15:22)

1. How do you respond to the idea of Sermon Club? Is this the kind of collaboration that you would like to incorporate into your life, or do you resist it? Why?

    _____

    _____

    _____

2. When have you seen Proverbs 15:22 to be true? Have you ever seen the opposite to be true? If so, when?

    _____

    _____

    _____

    _____

    _____

3. "Pride is what tells us that we understand the problem and have the solution without input from others." Do you agree or disagree that sinful pride is at work here? How is this relevant to your life?

_____

_____

_____

4. God often prefers to speak to us through others rather than directly to us. When has this been true in your experience? If the answer is never, what do you make of that?

_____

_____

_____

Day 3: Living like a Body

In **1 Corinthians 12,** Paul uses the image of a body to illustrate the relationships we are to have with others in the church. He wants us to see that the church is like a living body, and we are each like limbs or organs of that body. Some in the Corinthian church were saying, "Since I am not like you, I have no value." Others were saying, "Since you are not like me, you have no value." Paul wanted them to understand that some of us are eyes and others are feet, and both are valuable to the body's functioning. By working together, we can each contribute with the gifts we have been given.

The way we get involved in ministry is to look for ways to serve others. We see a need, and if we can help, we do. For instance, men who can fix an engine help those in the church who can't afford to pay a mechanic. Single moms can help each other with child care. Families and singles help each other move. Everyone can do something. Everyone's contributions are valued.

1. In the second paragraph of 1 Corinthians 12, Paul lists a few of the many gifts the Spirit gives to various members of Christ's body. Paul offers different lists of gifts in others of his letters. These lists are meant to be samples, not exhaustive. In the Old Testament, some workmen had the gift of shaping stone for the temple, while others had the gift of working with gold and silver. What other gifts can you think of that you have seen used by Christians in God's service?

   _____

   _____

   _____

   _____

2. In the fourth paragraph of the 1 Corinthians passage, Paul imagines what a foot might say because it isn't a hand. How

There are different kinds of gifts, but the same Spirit distributes them. There are different kinds of service, but the same Lord. There are different kinds of working, but in all of them and in everyone it is the same God at work.

Now to each one the manifestation of the Spirit is given for the common good. To one there is given through the Spirit a message of wisdom, to another a message of knowledge by means of the same Spirit, to another faith by the same Spirit, to another gifts of healing by that one Spirit, to another miraculous powers, to another prophecy, to another distinguishing between spirits, to another speaking in different kinds of tongues, and to still another the interpretation of tongues. All these are the work of one and the same Spirit, and he distributes them to each one, just as he determines.

Just as a body, though one, has many parts, but all its many parts form one body, so it is with Christ. For we were all baptized by one Spirit so as to form one body—whether Jews or Gentiles, slave or free—and we were all given the one Spirit to drink. Even so the body is not made up of one part but of many.

Now if the foot should say, "Because I am not a hand, I do not belong to the body," it would not for that reason stop being part of the body. And if the ear should say, "Because I am not an eye, I do not belong to the body," it would not for that reason stop being part of the body. If the whole body were an eye, where would the sense of hearing be? If the whole body were an ear, where would the sense of smell be? But in fact God has placed the parts in the body, every one of them, just as he wanted them to be. If they were all one part, where would the body be? As it is, there are many parts, but one body.

The eye cannot say to the hand, "I don't need you!" And the head cannot say to the feet, "I don't need you!" On the contrary, those parts of the body that seem to be weaker are indispensable, and the parts that we think are less honorable we treat with special honor. And the parts that are unpresentable are treated with special modesty, while our presentable parts need no special treatment. But God has put the body together, giving greater honor to the parts that lacked it, so that there should be no division in the body, but that its parts should have equal concern for each other. If one part suffers, every part suffers with it; if one part is honored, every part rejoices with it.
(1 Cor. 12:4–26)

is this like what a person might say? What is wrong with viewing yourself this way?

_____

_____

_____

3. In the fifth paragraph of the passage, Paul imagines what an eye might say to a hand. How is this like what a person might say, and for what reason? What is wrong with viewing other people this way?

_____

_____

_____

4. It seems so obvious that a diversity of organs is necessary for a human body. Why, then, are we often uncomfortable with diversity in the church?

_____

_____

_____

5. Paul says, "If one part suffers, every part suffers with it; if one part is honored, every part rejoices with it" (v. 26). Is this true in your experience of the church? If so, give an example. If not, why do you suppose it isn't?

_____

_____

_____

6. What opportunity do you have to suffer or rejoice with another Christian?

_____

_____

_____

Day 4: Using Your Gifts in the Body

Every body has a head. Christ is the head of His body, and He ultimately oversees the church. He appoints human overseers who serve in His place. These leaders discern which goals the church should take on together. Yesterday we talked about individual acts of service; today we'll talk about organized groups of servants using their gifts together.

For example, **Acts 6** recounts a situation in the early church where the Greek-speaking widows needed to be taken care of. Widows in that society were extremely vulnerable without a man to work for a living. The problem was brought to the elders (the apostles). They acknowledged the need and prayed about it. They understood that their role was to pray and teach, so others were needed to take care of the widows. They decided that the church should choose seven of its members who were filled with the Holy Spirit to handle the job. The people gave money so that the seven had something to give to the widows. The job was organized, and the seven were approved by the apostles.

In the same way, we today can bring issues to the leaders. We pray for the leaders, and we make ourselves available to be part of the solution, not just to point out the problem.

Some issues should be taken care of by individuals. All we have to do is see the need and help, or ask a few others to come and assist us to take care of the need. An illustration on taking the initiative: There was a cry for help from the railing of a cruise ship and people ran to see what had happened. A man had fallen overboard and was floundering in the water. One of the crew yelled, "Hold on, don't drown! I'll call a meeting of the crew and we'll decide how to best help you!"

We don't need to create a program for every problem. However, sometimes there is a need for an organized response. When that

In those days when the number of disciples was increasing, the Hellenistic Jews among them complained against the Hebraic Jews because their widows were being overlooked in the daily distribution of food. So the Twelve gathered all the disciples together and said, "It would not be right for us to neglect the ministry of the word of God in order to wait on tables. Brothers and sisters, choose seven men from among you who are known to be full of the Spirit and wisdom. We will turn this responsibility over to them and will give our attention to prayer and the ministry of the word." (Acts 6:1–4)

is the case, we submit the need to the leaders of the church and pray for a solution.

1. What are some of the needs in your church that require an organized response?

   _____
   _____
   _____

2. How are you participating in the solution of some need?

   _____
   _____
   _____

3. What is a need you've seen in someone's life that you were able to meet without involving a church program?

   _____
   _____
   _____

4. Do you feel that you're sufficiently involved in serving the needs of people around you or in your church? If so, what do you do? If not, what is a step you could take toward getting more plugged in to the service opportunities at your church?

   _____
   _____
   _____

Day 5: Togetherness Protects Us from "Me-ism"

If you prefer to solve problems and meet needs by yourself, more than likely you will experience pride attempting to sneak in to destroy you. Sometimes your solution hits the mark, and you alone get the credit. People pat you on the back, and the devil whispers, "You are important." You may easily get puffed up. Other times, when you don't understand the complexity of the problem and solution, your answer misses the mark and your effort fails. The devil whispers, "No one acknowledges your hard work. They don't appreciate you." Or "You are no good." Then you feel shame and a host of other self-centered emotions. Either way, the devil is playing with your pride, trying to drag you away from humility to thinking about yourself and your status. He wants you to think the situation is all about you. (See **1 Cor. 4:7**.)

Working with a team protects you from this pride problem. You share the solution, and God gets the glory.

Teamwork also protects you from overstressing yourself to the point of burnout. When you carry the job alone and your pride is on the line, you're tempted to push yourself harder than you can handle. Your life can become unbalanced as a spouse, an employee, or a ministry leader. With a genuine team, no one's ego is on the line. With a well-led team, nobody is pushed to the point of burnout and unbalance.

If you recognize that you have not been part of a team, then it's time to start praying and ask God and yourself why. Repentance must play a part in the change. To repent means you recognize that it has been wrong to be out of relationship with others. It means that you confess to the Lord that you have not been a part of the team, serving with your perspective and gifts. So many are critical because all they do is critique. A critical spirit is not discernment, and it's not a gift of the Holy Spirit. Repentance

For who makes you different from anyone else? What do you have that you did not receive? And if you did receive it, why do you boast as though you did not? (1 Cor. 4:7)

141

means that you have a change of heart that leads to a change of action. Then it's time to join a team.

There is plenty of ministry to be done. You might find a place on an existing team where you can offer your help and use your time and talents. Or you might identify a need that appears to be unmet by any ministry team. If your leadership is open to giving you ministry opportunities, begin to think about developing a team to meet the need, then approach your pastor or a designated leader with a plan: identify the need, list specifics about how you see that need being met, and explain how developing a team to address the need would help. Remember that the team not only meets the needs of others, but it also meets the relational needs of those on the team. When you get and give opportunities to be a part of what God is doing, it's a privilege and a blessing, so you don't need to be bashful about inviting others into something that will bless their lives. Be honest and share with your potential team that you're new at this and perhaps do not know how to do it very well and will make mistakes. Ask for grace, and when (not if) you make a mistake, don't be defensive—listen to and pray about what others say to you.

Don't allow the tasks of the ministry to crowd out developing a growing disciple-making relationship with the group. Begin to do life with those on the team. Pray together. Have dinner together. Have fun together. Go camping or to a park. Spend the first part of every gathering abiding in Christ. This means you read Scripture together and share your struggles and pray for one another, then begin the ministry task. When you serve, don't do it alone; take someone with you.

1. What are the benefits of teamwork that individual work doesn't offer?

   _____

   _____

   _____

2. Despite the benefits, many people still prefer to try to do things on their own. What do you think motivates them to

do that? What's the appeal of doing things solo? What role does pride play?

3. Have you experienced a ministry team? If so, what were the good aspects of that? What were the hard aspects?

4. Why do you think we frame the shift from solo ministry to team ministry as an issue of repentance? Where can sin often be found in solo ministry?

5. If you're not currently on a ministry team, what step toward joining or setting up a team could you take?

6. What are the key insights you have had in Week 7 of this study? What do you want to take from this week and apply to your life?

Growing Together

Day 1: Your group can be a place where you share a vision for every member growing to relational maturity. Talk about your vision, and see if others share it. How is your group already acting on such a vision?

Day 2: If you are an enthusiastic team player, that's great! If it's hard to build teamwork into your life, or if you resist doing so, your group should be a safe place to be honest about that. Others may be able to help you see what steps you can take toward integrating teammates into your life.

Day 3: Questions 4 through 6 are highly discussable with your group. Invite group members to share how people with different gifts, perspectives, or life experiences helped them when they were in pain or suffering, or how they were able to rejoice with each other.

Day 4: If there are people in your group who aren't currently involved in service opportunities, discussing question 4 can help them find opportunities that fit their abilities. But don't limit yourself to areas of service that are tailored for your gifts. If something needs to be done, pitch in and help.

Day 5: Discuss question 1. Question 5 revisits an issue from Day 4 in a slightly different way. In your group, help each other find ministry opportunities that will bring you together with others.

Check in on the accountability requests from Week 1.

Pray for those on Week 1's prayer list.

Week 8

Warmth on Cold, Dark Nights

Not only do we get a better return for our labor when we work together, but when we are together, we also receive strength to do the work long term.

The other day I was meeting with a young ministry team that had planted a church. They were using a model of ministry that moved everyone into serving the community through their home groups. They emphasized everyone using their gifts and meeting needs. However, as I asked questions, I could see that the team was tired. I applauded their desire to get people in the game—to bring glory to God by serving the hurting community together —but I shared with them that working together in ministry was not just a chance to do more and better work. A relational group (if honest and loving) is a means to fill up the cup emotionally and spiritually even as people are being poured out. It's essential to take time to fill your own cup; otherwise, you'll have nothing to give to your family or the rest of the team.

When I asked them what working together looked like as they had been doing it, they shared that they used their gifts and had great ideas. They got the encouragement that came from people who were astounded by the love they were receiving when they were hurting. It was giving them a chance to talk about theology and share their faith with potential disciples. I told them they were still missing something important: They were missing the opportunity to really share their struggles with one another—to do life with good friends. They were missing the opportunity to confess their sins and be healed, to share their doubts and be snatched from the fire. They were missing the strength that comes through the power of together in the Spirit. They were also missing the heart-to-heart times of fun that help knit relationships together.

When we serve together, if we open up our lives, we can experience far better than mere exhaustion. There is a time to just be together and do life together without serving the lost or hurting too. Jesus took His guys away to rest and pray. Ministry is a marathon, not a sprint. This week we'll focus on how we can take care of one another as we minister together.

Day 1: Never Alone

Ecclesiastes 4 tells us that we don't only do better work together—two are better than one, because they get a better return on their labor—but also that when one falls, the other can help him or her up. We all fall from time to time and need help to stand.

The passage goes on to say that while we are on the journey (presumably to do the work together), it gets cold at night. When one can't keep warm, two can keep each other warm. While we are on the mission of making disciples, we do better work together, yet there is a dark time, a cold time, and when it comes, we are more likely to get through it together. I don't think the writer is talking about just physical cold. I think he is talking about intimacy, warmth, and spiritual and emotional body heat that keeps us going. Relationship enables us to continue on the mission. It gives us spiritual strength to continue.

Jesus sent out His disciples by twos so that they could compensate in areas where their partner was weak in gifts but also give emotional and spiritual strength to each other.

A woman in our church who had been known as a servant began to be a no-show at the ministry where she had so faithfully served. For years she'd helped those who came to our church for food, and she walked them through the process of getting financial help. When she stopped coming around to serve, her friends pursued her to find out what was going on. When they finally caught up with her, she shared that she felt like she had nothing to give anymore because things had gotten tough at home with her husband and children. She felt her role was to help others, not to burden people with her problems.

Her friends let her know that she was wanted not just when she had a lot to give but also when she had nothing to give and needed to receive. A ministry team isn't about squeezing the last drop of service out of each person so that they collapse exhausted.

Two are better than one,
*   because they have a good return for*
*   their labor:*
If either of them falls down,
*   one can help the other up.*
But pity anyone who falls
*   and has no one to help them up.*
*   Also, if two lie down together,*
*   they will keep warm.*
But how can one keep warm alone?
*   Though one may be overpowered,*
two can defend themselves.
*   A cord of three strands is not quickly*
*   broken. (Eccles. 4:9–12)*

A ministry team pours into people so that they have something to give, and the team is there for them when life drains them and they need extra support.

1. Do the ministry teams at your church provide spiritual and emotional support to their members? If so, describe what they do. If not, why do you suppose they don't? (If you don't know because you're not on a ministry team, whom could you ask?)

   _____

   _____

   _____

2. What are the benefits of ministry teams that provide spiritual and emotional support to their members?

   _____

   _____

   _____

3. One way teams can support each other is to share prayer requests and pray for each other at the beginning of each task meeting. Why might it be helpful to do this at the beginning of meetings rather than at the end? Can you think of other ways a team could support one another?

   _____

   _____

   _____

   _____

4. What support do you need from others in the current season of your life?

   _____

   _____

   _____

   _____

Day 2: Being like Jesus

Jesus spent time with the masses, teaching and sharing stories. He also had an unknown number of disciples who followed Him and learned from Him things He didn't share with the crowd. Among these disciples were women who supported Him financially (**Luke 8:1–3**). He also had friends who didn't travel with Him, such as Lazarus and his sisters Mary and Martha (**Luke 10:38–39; John 12:1–3**). From His larger circle of disciples, He chose twelve to be apostles, and these twelve got to know Him especially well. And even among the Twelve, three men were His closest friends: Peter and the sons of Zebedee (James and John). He was real with all of these people, but He was especially real and vulnerable with Peter, James, and John. John seems to have been closer to Him than anyone.

Jesus, of course, was making disciples who could make disciples, but He was also modeling relationship for His followers to see. Jesus did ministry and life with people, and we have the Gospels to show us what that looked like. I believe He gained strength even from His disciples, especially those He was closest to. He allowed them to see how He trusted in the Father and even how He struggled. Jesus shared His struggle with his friends and asked them to pray for Him as He pled with the Father to take the cup from Him. He shared that His soul was grieved to the point of death (**Matt. 26:36–38**).

So many pastors tell me they can't reveal themselves to anyone in their church because their people wouldn't understand or would judge them and they would lose their credibility. However, Jesus revealed Himself to mere humans, so the excuse doesn't work for us—there is a much larger gap between us and God than there is between us and people in our church. He didn't reveal Himself to everyone, but He had a few flawed but good friends whom He trusted to know Him.

After this, Jesus traveled about from one town and village to another, proclaiming the good news of the kingdom of God. The Twelve were with him, and also some women who had been cured of evil spirits and diseases: Mary (called Magdalene) from whom seven demons had come out; Joanna the wife of Chuza, the manager of Herod's household; Susanna; and many others. These women were helping to support them out of their own means. (Luke 8:1–3)

As Jesus and his disciples were on their way, he came to a village where a woman named Martha opened her home to him. She had a sister called Mary, who sat at the Lord's feet listening to what he said. (Luke 10:38–39)

Six days before the Passover, Jesus came to Bethany, where Lazarus lived, whom Jesus had raised from the dead. Here a dinner was given in Jesus' honor. Martha served, while Lazarus was among those reclining at the table with him. Then Mary took about a pint of pure nard, an expensive perfume; she poured it on Jesus' feet and wiped his feet with her hair. And the house was filled with the fragrance of the perfume. (John 12:1–3)

Then Jesus went with his disciples to a place called Gethsemane, and he said to them, "Sit here while I go over there and pray." He took Peter and the two sons of Zebedee along with him, and he began to be sorrowful and troubled. Then he said to them, "My soul is overwhelmed with sorrow to the point of death. Stay here and keep watch with me." (Matt. 26:36–38)

Jesus makes it clear to us that, yes, we are on mission, but the mission is shared. We minister to one another in the midst of mission so that the work is continued. God works through others to empower us to persevere.

1. Read Matthew 26:36–38 in the margin. What does Jesus say to His three friends? What can we learn about Him from His willingness to say this to them?

_____

_____

_____

2. Peter, James, and John were flawed men. Peter tried to talk Jesus out of going to the cross (Matt. 16:21–23). James and John tried to maneuver Jesus into giving them the places of greatest power in His kingdom (20:20–28). All three of them fell asleep when He asked them to pray with Him just before His arrest (26:40–45). Yet He didn't tell Himself they were too flawed to be His friends and know His heart. Knowing they would let Him down, He still made Himself vulnerable. Why do you think He did this? What is the lesson for us?

_____

_____

_____

3. Do you have friends who get to know the real you, who support you spiritually and are supported by you? If so, how do you support each other? If not, why not?

_____

_____

_____

4. How does it affect you to think of Jesus relying on those flawed people to be His friends?

_____

_____

_____

Day 3: Help for the Struggling

Jesus shared Himself with those around Him. He revealed His frustration at times. He wept for Mary and Martha when He saw their grief at their brother's death. He was in such distress when He prayed in Gethsemane before His arrest that "his sweat was like drops of blood falling to the ground" (Luke 22:44).

If Jesus needed the support of His Father and friends, we need it much more. We need it not just for times of trouble but also for times of temptation. We need honest and transparent relationship if we are to defeat sin in our lives.

James 5:16 tells us that we must confess our sins one to another if we are to be healed. In this passage the word for "sins" means shortcomings, deficiencies. Notice that there is power to heal when we are honest about where we are struggling.

In **Jude 22–23** we are told to be merciful to those who doubt and to help snatch them from the fire. How different this is from the attitude common in America that we must be perfect, never struggling with sin or doubt. This attitude is harmful because we all struggle. We are told to snatch others from the fire, but without real relationship we don't know who is doubting and who is in the fire. Going to church once a week doesn't allow us to know what is really happening beneath the surface. Being at church once a week doesn't allow the time and the atmosphere of honesty to tell each other what is really going on.

Also, some people drift into sin and don't seem to realize it. Unless someone really knows us and has spent enough time with us to see the subtle shifts, then how can they help us?

Finally, some think that their job is to help others, but they won't be honest about their own struggles. They think they are less mature if they can't go it alone. This is tragically false. Mature Christians give and receive—they help when they are able, and they are also honest about their own needs, because they know God

Therefore confess your sins to each other and pray for each other so that you may be healed. The prayer of a righteous person is powerful and effective. (James 5:16)

Be merciful to those who doubt; save others by snatching them from the fire. (Jude 22–23)

blesses the humble. When we need help, God seldom answers our prayers by having us win the lottery or strike oil in our backyards like the Beverly Hillbillies. Instead, He answers prayers through other believers. It's actually the spiritually immature person who does not accept or seek a spiritual family support system because he is too busy or too walled off emotionally. It's the immature person who will not communicate and will not let others love him by caring for his needs.

Repeatedly, I deal with this kind of sad situation: A couple comes for counseling. They have been Christians for years. The marital struggle has gone on for a long time, but they've carried the burdens alone and they are exhausted and ready to give up. They haven't shared their problems with mature believers. Oftentimes they take advice from non-Christians or from far-removed television counselors or even from soap operas, and the counsel doesn't line up with God's plan. After trying everything but seeking counsel from godly friends, they tell me I am the last hope, and if I can't help, they are done. They began falling long ago. Now, over time, hearts are hardened and emotional wounds are infected. Their spiritual lives are shallow, and we have a problem that I am not sure either of them has the spiritual strength or desire to do what it will take to fix.

What is sad about couples like this is that often they have had mature Christian friends along the way who would have listened and given godly counsel had they been honest. But whenever they were asked about their lives or marriage, they gave the old standby answer, "I am fine." Their friends are left to think that the couple was doing all right—but they weren't.

1. What's the purpose of confessing your sins, temptations, and doubts to mature believers?

   _____

   _____

   _____

2. How would confessing their struggles to a mature Christian help a couple with marriage troubles before it's too late to save the marriage?

3. What do you think keeps people from looking for trustworthy fellow believers to whom they can open up about their temptations and doubts? If you've done this yourself, what are your reasons?

4. What are your sins, temptations, or doubts? You won't have to share them with your small group. Write them down, though, so that you can look at them and really own up to them.

5. Did you write down anything that you would benefit from sharing with a mature believer? If so, who could you talk to?

Day 4: Big Rocks

Then he told them many things in parables, saying: "A farmer went out to sow his seed. As he was scattering the seed, some fell along the path, and the birds came and ate it up. Some fell on rocky places, where it did not have much soil. It sprang up quickly, because the soil was shallow. But when the sun came up, the plants were scorched, and they withered because they had no root. Other seed fell among thorns, which grew up and choked the plants. Still other seed fell on good soil, where it produced a crop—a hundred, sixty or thirty times what was sown. Whoever has ears, let them hear." (Matt. 13:3–9)

In **Matthew 13:3–9**, Jesus tells the story of the four soils. In each case, the soil stands for the heart of a person and the seed the gospel message. The path is hard-packed soil, too hard for the seed to penetrate even a little bit. The devil snatches that seed away. But in the other three cases, the soil seemingly accepts the seed and begins to grow a spiritual plant.

In the rocky soil, the roots of the gospel plant dive down deep and encounter the rocks. I believe that every person who seems to receive the seed of God's Word will experience this: the roots of the plant will push down and hit rocks (sin, strongholds of the enemy, broken perspectives). God's Word is used by the Holy Spirit to convict us for our good. In every soil there are rocks. The question is, what the person will do when, like a seedling of God's kingdom, they face the challenge of a rock. Likewise, every soil has thorns that have always been there or have been planted by the enemy to choke out the gospel seed. Soil has enough nutrients to sustain only so much, and the enemy loves to sow distractions that will take away from the wheat planted that can grow much spiritual fruit. The question is what the person will do when the gospel plant tangles with thorns. Trouble, persecution, the worries of this life, the deceitfulness of wealth—these happen to all of us. The question is what we do when we encounter these rocks and thorny distractors. The good soil is the person who decides he or she wants the plant God has planted enough to dig out the rocks and thorns.

I also believe that some rocks are so big and some thorns are so deeply rooted that only with the help of a brother or sister can we get the rocks and the thorns out of our soil. This is why Paul tells us in Galatians 6:2 to carry one another's burdens. In my yard I had big rocks and needed help to move them. I had thornbushes I thought were trees. I needed an expert friend of mine to come and help me know what I was looking at, and then the problems were big enough that we had to pull them out together. (In some cases we needed a tractor.)

So often God's Word, with our help, reveals that people have a thornbush or a rock, and they acknowledge it. But then we don't help them come to grips with it and pull it out. We don't carry their burden with them. Sure, they must do their part, and we can't do it for them, but often it takes more than one person to get the bitter root or stronghold of the enemy out. At other times someone points out that we have a thornbush or a rock getting in the way of progress in our lives, but we like it right where it is. Instead, we need to let the spiritually mature help us identify what is what and then help us deal with it. And when we see someone in the body of Christ with something too big to carry alone, we need to help them carry it (**Gal. 6:2**).

1. Review Matthew 13:3–9 again, and read **Matthew 13:18–23**. What does the rocky soil represent? The thorny soil?

   _____

   _____

   _____

2. Which of these have been problems in your life? How so? Which are problems now?

   _____

   _____

   _____

3. Have you ever had help digging a rock or a thornbush out of your soil? If so, describe the help. If not, why do you think you haven't?

   _____

   _____

   _____

4. Are you close enough to anyone to see rocks or thorns in their lives? If so, what would motivate you to help them with that? Or what would make you not want to offer help?

Carry each other's burdens, and in this way you will fulfill the law of Christ. (Gal. 6:2)

Listen then to what the parable of the sower means: When anyone hears the message about the kingdom and does not understand it, the evil one comes and snatches away what was sown in their heart. This is the seed sown along the path. The seed falling on rocky ground refers to someone who hears the word and at once receives it with joy. But since they have no root, they last only a short time. When trouble or persecution comes because of the word, they quickly fall away. The seed falling among the thorns refers to someone who hears the word, but the worries of this life and the deceitfulness of wealth choke the word, making it unfruitful. But the seed falling on good soil refers to someone who hears the word and understands it. This is the one who produces a crop, yielding a hundred, sixty or thirty times what was sown. (Matt. 13:18–23)

_____

_____

_____

_____

5. If you're not close enough to anyone to see their rocks and thorns, what would it take for you to get close enough?

_____

_____

_____

6. What could keep you from getting close enough?

_____

_____

_____

7. Is your group a safe place for you to open up about the rocks and thorns in your soil? Would you want someone in your group to tell you how they see rocks or thorns affecting you? Why or why not? If someone saw you wrapped up in the deceitfulness of wealth, for example, would you want them to tell you? Let your group know what your desires are in this area.

_____

_____

_____

Day 5: God's Part, My Part, Their Part

I often have people pour themselves into others, but after a time, they are frustrated at themselves, thinking they have failed, because the person they have been trying to help is not changing. I tell them there are three parts of the helping process: God's part, the other person's part, and our part. We can't do God's part or their part; we can only do our part. If we try to do God's part, we will fail. If we try to do their part, we are enabling them to stay immature and stuck. We can help someone identify the thornbush or the rock; we can even help them dig it out if they will let us and then they do their part (**Gal. 6:2, 5**). But we cannot do it for them.

Carry each other's burdens, and in this way you will fulfill the law of Christ. . . . For each one should carry their own load. (Gal. 6:2, 5)

A young volunteer couple who worked with marriages shared with me their story. The husband had had an affair, and through the hard recovery process, he accepted Christ. He had wrecked his life and his wife's life, and this had caused a huge change in his life. They had both grown incredibly, and now they were mentoring couples who were going through the same thing.

The husband became very emotional as he shared with me all that he and his wife had poured into the couples in his group. He had come to their houses at midnight. He had answered calls and led groups. And now he asked me, "What am I doing wrong? They aren't changing. I feel like a failure. I feel like God must be upset with me."

I pointed out to them that they were currently giving more than most I knew. They were walking with Jesus personally and together as a couple—very stable. They were sharing hard truth but doing it in love, but these couples were not changing. I reminded them that Jesus had not done anything wrong, and still the disciples left Him and even betrayed Him. I said the greatest Father in history lost His two children in the Garden of Eden.

Free will is a tough thing to deal with. If you are facing a crisis in your local church, group, or home, you need to remember that just because God is doing His part and we are doing our part does not mean the person in crisis will do their part and your efforts will be successful. People have to choose: Will they submit to the Lord and obey? Will they take the responsibility that is theirs? They have to carry their burden with us. We can't do it for them.

My son is now a youth minister, but when he was younger he went through two rehab centers and a homeless shelter. We tried everything we could think of to do our part, but nothing seemed to work. I almost resigned over it, but my friend came alongside me and helped my wife and me to carry our burden together. It was so good not to be judged but to be encouraged by believers in our church and family. The hardest thing we ever did was leave our son in the homeless shelter for almost four months. We had to make the hard decision to step back and allow him to start paying the consequences of his own choices. We couldn't do it for him, and we finally realized it. If we never let him hit the bottom, then he would never fully feel the effects of what he was doing. When he finally started doing his part, we again jumped in to do the part we could do.

Our role is to help one another, but sometimes helping is to step back and let God do His part and work on the person. Honestly, when we love someone, that is the hardest thing to do, because what is killing them is killing us. And they don't see that it is killing them.

I told the ministry couple who came to me, "God is proud of you. He will continue to work. Do your part, and remember, sometimes we are only planting seeds that later will come to fruition. You may think what you are doing isn't working, but you won't know until much later."

1. In the case of the couple ministering to other couples in troubled marriages, what is God's part? What is the ministering couple's part? What is the part of the couples in crisis?

   _____

   _____

   _____

2. In the case of a drug- or alcohol-addicted adult, what is God's part? What is the addict's part? What is his parents' part, if they want to be helpful?

_____

_____

_____

3. Why is it often hard to discern our part in these situations? How would seeking help from a mature Christian benefit you?

_____

_____

_____

4. What can help us discern our job? How might our relationships with our local church, our group, a mature Christ-follower, a mature family member, or a counselor help us?

_____

_____

_____

5. What are the key insights you have had in Week 8 of this study? What do you want to take from this week and apply to your life?

_____

_____

_____

Growing Together

Look ahead to Week 9, and decide if that will be your final meeting or if your group would like an optional Week 10 for review and celebration.

Day 1: Question 4 will lead your group right into your prayer time. Be sure to give everyone in the group a chance to answer it. By now there shouldn't be anyone in the group who says he or she doesn't need any support.

Day 2: When your group discusses question 3, hopefully you'll be able to say that the people in your group are becoming friends like this. If not, what could your group do better?

Day 3: Questions 4 and 5 are not for group discussion unless you are in a small accountability group that is a safe place to be completely open. What you can discuss with a larger group is, "Did questions 4 and 5 lead you to any fruitful chance to be open with another believer? If so, talk about what has been helpful."

Day 4: Hopefully your group has become a safe place to be honest and vulnerable. Discuss your answers to question 7 in as much depth as you feel comfortable.

Day 5: If you are in a situation and are having trouble discerning your part and the other person's part, consider taking it to your group for their feedback. Be careful about using names or details if confidentiality is necessary in order to avoid gossip. Share some key insights from the week.

Check in on the accountability requests from Week 1.

Pray for those on Week 1's prayer list.

Week 9

Protecting One Another

As we've unpacked Ecclesiastes 4, we've seen that it's a miserable business to be alone. We were made for relationship, which leads to a better return for our work in fulfilling the mission for which we were saved (to make disciples). As we progress along the journey together, we will each inevitably struggle at times and even fall. We are fallible, but with help we can get back up. Pity the one who falls with no one there to help him up. Along the way it will get cold, and relationship (emotional and spiritual intimacy) keeps us warm. It gives us emotional and spiritual stamina to withstand the rigors of the journey.

Now **Ecclesiastes 4:12** goes on to tell us that when one is alone, he or she can be defeated by an enemy. But with two (or even better, three or more), there is protection and safety. This is our focus for this week—facing our common enemy in unity and relationship, never in isolation.

Notice, by the way, that this passage is not saying, "If perchance you happen to encounter an enemy, you will need help." It's saying we absolutely *do* have a fight on our hands, and we win when we fight together and for one another.

One of the ways we prepare for battle is by helping each other to daily fasten on our spiritual armor. Just as 1 Corinthians 13 is not a marriage text, so Ephesians 6:10–20 is not an individual text. It is written to the church. Paul understood Roman armor well, as he saw it everywhere he went. The people of that time would have understood it as well. Some of the armor could not be put

Though one may be overpowered, two can defend themselves. A cord of three strands is not quickly broken. (Eccles. 4:12)

on by yourself—it tied in the back—so each of us needs fellow warriors to help us secure the breastplate of faith, straighten the helmet of salvation, cinch up the belt of truth, lift the heavy sword of the Spirit, and so on. Not only do we need someone to teach us how to use it and put it on in the first place, we continue to need fellow soldiers to help us put the armor on no matter how many battles we have been through.

What is more, out there on the field we watch each other's back, or we're doomed. We daily face a spiritual enemy. He has trained his army to divide and isolate us. But no matter how resolved are the armies of hell to stop us, as *the church united* we can't lose.

So let's get out there. Together!

Day 1: The Battle Is On!

Battle? What battle?

The world, and even some Christians, mock us when we speak of the reality of spiritual warfare. Hollywood often puts out horror movies with demonic undertones, but they don't actually believe the devil exists any more than Freddy Krueger does. Those who actually believe in demonic forces or speak of interacting with them at all are seen as ignorant or mentally unstable. Christians who speak in "militant" terms are presumed intolerant and summarily judged as uneducated and unfeeling. Some consider us dangerous.

That's exactly the way Satan wants it.

One of his main tactics is the ambush. An ambush works when the person is unaware of the potential enemy lurking. But no one who gives the Bible a serious reading can possibly avoid the fact of the history-spanning conflict. It dwarfs any mere world war in scope and stakes. Earth's nations fight for territories, even continents. But the spiritual forces for good and for evil have been vying since Eden for the eternal destiny of all humanity.

You and I are part of this war. We didn't have to sign up or be drafted. We're all born into it, and we're fighting—every minute of every day. We're reminded of it throughout Scripture, as Paul does when he addresses our attitude and approach toward others (**2 Tim. 2:24–26**).

But somehow even we Jesus-followers have trouble remembering this invisible, ongoing reality. We let our own wishes and expectations, along with the persuasive alliance of the world and Satan, fool us into believing that our greatest goal should be personal and immediate ease. We want to live in a "fair," pain-free world, so we set our sights on accomplishing this and avoiding any roadblocks to it. And when Jesus doesn't protect us from battles and injuries that result—some of which we inflict on ourselves—we get upset. Deepest disappointment is the result of the most unrealistic expectations.

And the Lord's servant must not be quarrelsome but must be kind to everyone, able to teach, not resentful. Opponents must be gently instructed, in the hope that God will grant them repentance leading them to a knowledge of the truth, and that they will come to their senses and escape from the trap of the devil, who has taken them captive to do his will. (2 Tim. 2:24–26)

Do not suppose that I have come to bring peace to the earth. I did not come to bring peace, but a sword. For I have come to turn

"*a man against his father,*

a daughter against her mother,

a daughter-in-law against her mother-in-law—

a man's enemies will be the members of his own household."

(Matt. 10:34–36)

Walk by the Spirit, and you will not gratify the desires of the flesh. . . . They are in conflict with each other, so that you are not to do whatever you want. (Gal. 5:16–17)

Timothy, my son . . . fight the good fight, keeping faith and a good conscience, which some have rejected and suffered shipwreck in regard to their faith. (1 Tim. 1:18–19 NASB)

I have fought the good fight, I have finished the race, I have kept the faith. . . . The Lord stood at my side and gave me strength, so that through me the message might be fully proclaimed and all the Gentiles might hear it. And I was delivered from the lion's mouth. The Lord will rescue me from every evil attack and will bring me safely to his heavenly kingdom. (2 Tim. 4:7, 17–18)

You adulterous people, don't you know that friendship with the world

Jesus never softened the difficult truth. He mercifully went out of His way to wake us from our dreamland: "You are under attack. Stay alert! Your enemy is vicious. He will even turn your own family against you." (See **Matt. 10:34–36**.)

It is the mature Jesus-follower who lives in consistent awareness of the threat. Just as effective armies study to know their enemies' weapons and methods, so also effective spiritual warriors scour the Scriptures to understand our adversary's tools and tactics.

Scripture tells us he lies (his method) and he murders (his goal). And he isn't stupid. He's a clever schemer, and he will wield any weapon or way that does the job. Intimidation or subtlety, half-truth or lie, beauty or ugliness, pride or shame. He knows how to use any of them to create confusion, to steal the light out of the room and leave you in darkness.

And isolation is his favorite method. He knows that we were not built to be alone, and just as importantly, none of us can thrive alone. He knows that when we are isolated, he can distort the truth without any interference from others. When we're alone, he can either puff us up with pride, which ultimately kills our relationship with God and others, or he drives us into the ground with guilt and shame, which again keeps us separated from God and others.

1. From the **six passages** listed in the margin, beginning with **Galatians 5**, describe the battle in which we all engage daily. (Note, by the way, that Scripture identifies more than one enemy.)

   _____

   _____

   _____

2. Describe a few ways you have noticed and experienced a spiritual battle going on in your life.

   _____

   _____

   _____

Once we understand God's strategy for our unity and maturity, we can also easily predict the devil's strategy to thwart God. God's strategy to reclaim us is rooted in relationship (Eph. 4:11–16), so our enemy naturally seeks to destroy our connections with our Father and with each other.

As we have discovered throughout this journey, in God's eyes it is not good for us to be alone—two are better than one—so we are commanded not to forsake the gathering together of the believers.

And when you gather, don't "hide in plain sight." Choose to take relational risks with trustworthy people. It's God's strategy for victory over sin and for your ultimate happiness.

3. Satan will use a variety of weapons to destroy your desire and capacity to have the relationships you were designed to need. Listed below are some of the ways the devil creates barriers. For each of Satan's isolating tactics, identify one counterstrategy. Beginning with **Ephesians 4**, use the next **five passages** in the margin to help you. How must fellow Christians be part of each counterstrategy?

Unforgiveness (prideful insistence on being right, punishing those who've wronged us by withholding relationship with them)

_____

_____

_____

Distraction (forgetting our innate need for each other and keeping too busy to spend time on what matters most)

_____

_____

_____

Discouragement (personal failure that makes us not believe we are capable of having what we need, combined with disbelief that anyone else can help)

_____

_____

_____

Doubt (assuming the worst about others; skepticism about God's ability to work through others)

_____

_____

_____

means enmity against God? Therefore, anyone who chooses to be a friend of the world becomes an enemy of God. . . . Submit yourselves, then, to God. Resist the devil, and he will flee from you. (James 4:4, 7)

Dear friends, I warn you as "temporary residents and foreigners" to keep away from worldly desires that wage war against your very souls. (1 Pet. 2:11 NLT)

You, dear children, are from God and have overcome them, because the one who is in you is greater than the one who is in the world. . . . Everyone born of God overcomes the world. This is the victory that has overcome the world, even our faith. Who is it that overcomes the world? Only the one who believes that Jesus is the Son of God. (1 John 4:4; 5:4–5)

Be kind and compassionate to one another, forgiving each other, just as in Christ God forgave you. (Eph. 4:32)

And let us consider how we may spur one another on toward love and good deeds, not giving up meeting together, as some are in the habit of doing, but encouraging one another—and all the more as you see the Day approaching. (Heb. 10:24–25)

He who began a good work in you will carry it on to completion until the day of Christ Jesus. (Phil. 1:6)

Therefore confess your sins to each other and pray for each other so that you may be healed. The prayer of a righteous person is powerful and effective. (James 5:16)

Who is wise and understanding among you? Let them show it by their good life, by deeds done in the humility that comes from wisdom. (James 3:13)

Whoever isolates himself seeks his own desire;
he breaks out against all sound judgment. (Prov. 18:1 ESV)

Fear (letting past pain convince us that we must never let others hurt us again)

_____

_____

_____

Self-righteousness (moral superiority, distancing ourselves from second-class saints)

_____

_____

_____

Isolation keeps us buying the lies; the lies lead us to believe isolation is best. The devil's lies sound like our own thoughts, so they're hard to recognize as coming from outside. And if we hear something enough, we can end up adopting a line of reasoning ourselves, without further help from the enemy. (See **Prov. 18:1**.)

To me, the devil is the lawn mower man. Old lawn mowers have a pull string, and sometimes you have to pull them multiple times before the engine takes off. The devil likes to pull the string by telling me I am no good—or too good; either of which can lead to isolation from others. Before long, if I allow the devil to speak enough, I—like the lawn mower—will take off and end up chopping everything in my path to bits.

True and right thinking leads to true and right living. Which is why we are told that we must be transformed by the renewing of our minds. When you recognize that something isn't right in your life (sometimes brought to light by a caring brother or sister in Christ), take it to the Lord and ask forgiveness. There will be times, however, when the accuser of the brethren will accuse you of something that is not true. God's Word, His Spirit living in you, and godly people you are in relationship with are there to counter these lies. Pray for truth, and your Father is sure to provide it. Pursue truth, and you will catch it. Accept truth, revealed in the Bible and embodied in your faithful brothers and sisters.

4. Following is a list of common lies the devil uses to persuade us to choose isolation. For each one, identify a biblical

antidote—that is, at least one corresponding truth you find in Scripture. Use the **eight passages** in the margin to help you.

Guilt

"You feel guilty, so you must *be* guilty." "God's forgiveness isn't for you or you would feel it." "God knows what you have thought and done, and there is no way He can forgive you. If anyone else knew what you have done and thought, they would agree."

_____

_____

_____

Shame

"You were born unforgivable." "You're damaged beyond saving." "If people knew what you were really like, they would be disgusted."

_____

_____

_____

Despair/Surrender

"Don't bother anyone else with your problems; you're hopeless." "You're a loser; you can't win." "They are too busy to help and wouldn't understand anyway."

_____

_____

_____

Pride

"You're better than them." "You're weak if you depend on others." "Only weak people need crutches. You can do it yourself."

_____

_____

_____

Self-pity/Self-justification

"Your battle is unwinnable—harder than anyone else's." "No one else has it as bad as you do, so they couldn't possibly understand." "If they were dealing with what you are

Therefore, there is now no condemnation for those who are in Christ Jesus, because through Christ Jesus the law of the Spirit who gives life has set you free from the law of sin and death. (Rom. 8:1)

Who will bring any charge against those whom God has chosen? It is God who justifies. Who then is the one who condemns? No one. Christ Jesus who died—more than that, who was raised to life—is at the right hand of God and is also interceding for us. (Rom. 8:33–34)

For those God foreknew he also predestined to be conformed to the image of his Son, that he might be the firstborn among many brothers and sisters. And those he predestined, he also called; those he called, he also justified; those he justified, he also glorified.

What, then, shall we say in response to these things? If God is for us, who can be against us? (Rom. 8:29–31)

Therefore, as God's chosen people, holy and dearly loved . . . (Col. 3:12)

In order to keep me from becoming conceited, I was given a thorn in my flesh, a messenger of Satan, to torment me. Three times I pleaded with the Lord to take it away from me. But he

said to me, "My grace is sufficient for you, for my power is made perfect in weakness." Therefore I will boast all the more gladly about my weaknesses, so that Christ's power may rest on me. That is why, for Christ's sake, I delight in weaknesses, in insults, in hardships, in persecutions, in difficulties. For when I am weak, then I am strong. (2 Cor. 12:7–10)

Now if the foot should say, "Because I am not a hand, I do not belong to the body," it would not for that reason stop being part of the body. (1 Cor. 12:15)

The eye cannot say to the hand, "I don't need you!" And the head cannot say to the feet, "I don't need you!" (1 Cor. 12:21)

No temptation has overtaken you except what is common to mankind. And God is faithful; he will not let you be tempted beyond what you can bear. But when you are tempted, he will also provide a way out so that you can endure it. (1 Cor. 10:13)

dealing with, then they would do what you are doing too." "Everyone messes up in some way, so you are justified to blow it the way you did."

_____

_____

Discontent

"Doing the right thing shouldn't be this hard." "The fact that this doesn't work easily means that there is something better out there for you."

_____

_____

_____

5. How do the truths you wrote for question 4 lead you back into relationships with God and others?

_____

_____

_____

6. In your group this week, share which lie the devil uses to bring about your downfall the most. How could the group help you overcome that lie?

_____

_____

_____

7. What could someone else say or do to help you have victory when you are doing battle with the enemy?

_____

_____

_____

8. What could someone say that would not be helpful? Can you think of a time when someone was trying to help you but instead made things worse? What happened?

_____

_____

_____

Day 2: Blow the Trumpet!

One of the great stories in the Bible is about Nehemiah and his mission to rescue ruined Jerusalem. Israel had persisted in unfaithfulness to God, so He had allowed another nation to conquer their country and take the people into exile. Decades later, God prompted the Persian king to let the Jews return to their land.

Nehemiah was appointed governor and led an expedition back to his homeland. He put the people to work rebuilding Jerusalem's wall. But non-Jews had settled comfortably into the vacant land decades before, and they didn't take well to this influx of returning Jews—whom they despised. They were terrified at the possibility of a fortified Jerusalem, and they tried every tactic to stop the rebuilding. When dirty politics didn't work, the bullies started threatening military attacks against the nearly defenseless Jews.

1. Read **Nehemiah 4:14, 16–20** and explain Nehemiah's wise plan for the people's coordination for mutual defense.

   _____

   _____

   _____

Nehemiah's promise to the Jews is also God's promise to us: When we blow the trumpet, we all rally together and remember, "Our God will fight for us!" When we battle evil in each other's defense, God is working through us to fight and win.

While the people were doing their work, Nehemiah gave them two responsibilities:

a. To blow the trumpet if they were under attack.

b. To listen and rally to the trumpet for defensive support.

The rest of Week 9 spells out both sides of this warfare-in-relationship plan as it applies to Jesus followers today.

I stood up and said to the nobles, the officials and the rest of the people, "Don't be afraid of them. Remember the Lord, who is great and awesome, and fight for your families, your sons and your daughters, your wives and your homes." . . . From that day on, half of my men did the work, while the other half were equipped with spears, shields, bows and armor. The officers posted themselves behind all the people of Judah who were building the wall. Those who carried materials did their work with one hand and held a weapon in the other, and each of the builders wore his sword at his side as he worked. But the man who sounded the trumpet stayed with me.

Then I said to the nobles, the officials and the rest of the people, "The work is extensive and spread out, and we are widely separated from each other along the wall. Wherever you hear the sound of the trumpet, join us there. Our God will fight for us." (Neh. 4:14, 16–20)

Today, blowing the trumpet means reaching out to other believers and saying, "Hey, I'm under attack and need support!" It means calling out for prayer, guidance, and encouragement.

2. Look back at questions 3 through 7 of yesterday's study. As you resist the enemy's lies and strategies, how is the defensive support of other believers—including those in your small group—important for you?

_____

_____

_____

See to it, brothers and sisters, that none of you has a sinful, unbelieving heart that turns away from the living God. But encourage one another daily, as long as it is called "Today," so that none of you may be hardened by sin's deceitfulness. (Heb. 3:12–13)

3. **Hebrews 3:12–13** says to "encourage one another daily . . . so that none of you may be hardened by sin's deceitfulness." What sort of encouragement do you need to keep from being hardened?

_____

_____

_____

4. What do you think keeps people from blowing the trumpet when they need encouragement to stay away from sin or some other lie from the enemy?

_____

_____

_____

We thwart sin's deceitfulness together, in partnership—truth seeking and truth telling. We can't watch our own backs.

Yet many Jesus-followers fall silently under attack. We think it's weak to need help, mature to win alone. But alone, we lose. In silence we succumb. And we can even resent the fact that no one came to our aid when we did not make it clear that we even had a need. Sometimes we think it should be obvious to others that we're struggling, but it's not. Even worse, we can live our lives without being a part of a spiritual army, and our trials can reveal that we have not built relationships that can help because we have been too distracted.

Test your movie-viewing recall—and your openness to others' help—as you consider each of these characters:

5. *Spider-Man:* I do life alone. When I let anyone close, they hurt me and I hurt them. It's best for everyone this way. *Why is this a faulty, immature attitude?*

----

6. *Luke Skywalker:* I have a relationship with God, and even help others with their struggles. His job for me is rescuing, not being rescued. His sufficiency keeps me from needing anything from others. It's me and Jesus. *Why is this a faulty, immature attitude?*

----

7. *Nameless Bystander #26:* I'm the helpless mother with the stroller, the child on the bike, the nerdy businessman. I live under crumbling bridges and in dilapidated busses. I always cross the street at exactly the wrong time. I am a nobody. Don't bother looking for me in the closing credits; I'm of no use to anyone. *What fact or facts of God's reality is this person missing?*

The mature movie hero is the Avengers team that says, "Each of us needs his or her super(natural) powers (in relationship with God), but we also need each other. We abide in Christ and in deep relationships with Jesus-followers. Listening with care and sharing openly are both commitments for everyone. God works through the others to help the one, and each one welcomes help from others and from God."

8. How has your small group helped each other with the struggles or problems the group members have faced? Note some examples.

_____

_____

_____

_____

_____

Day 3: Rally to the Trumpet!

Soldiering in relationship can only work when all of us are committed to both responsibilities—blowing the trumpet for help and rallying to the trumpet to provide support. Yesterday we contemplated blowing the trumpet; today we'll look at how we respond when we hear one blown.

Let's revisit Nehemiah and the rebuilding of Jerusalem. Imagine the real possibility that several independent-minded families were so busy working on the wall and protecting their own homes that they didn't pay attention to Nehemiah and his plan. These would be the do-it-yourselfers, the mavericks, those who lived by the philosophy, "Take care of yourself, because no one else has your back, and honestly I don't need them to." They heard that Nehemiah had mapped out a cooperative plan, but these self-sufficient types skipped the meeting. They saw no need to work together. So when the trumpet sounded, they kept on working, taking care of themselves. Alone. Their neighbors didn't get the help they needed, so they were defeated. The mavericks never expected that allowing their neighbors to fall would mean that the enemy was now in the city. The enemy had no plans of stopping, and now there was a problem within and without—the defenders were surrounded. Those who failed to help their neighbors were now alone and outnumbered. The family they could have helped would have been there for them when they were the next target.

1. Following are three biblical reasons for following the Nehemiah plan today. Describe the benefits of respecting each one and the dangers of neglecting them.

   • Submission to God-given authority. (For example, your pastor blows the trumpet on someone's behalf.)

   _____

   _____

   _____

- Mission—your church is meant to shine in the world as a unified city of refuge.

- Love for neighbors under attack.

Ignoring others' cries for help reveals emotional and spiritual immaturity—a lack of love and a lack of shared purpose and mission. In today's life-and-death battle, this is how people die spiritually. It allows the enemy inside our walls to harm us.

As a soldier who is watching the backs of your comrades in battle, keep your eyes and ears open, alert to respond when they ask for help. Even more than that, look for changes in the way they are acting and spending their time. You can tell a heart is changing when priorities are changing. Sometimes people don't even know they are being funneled by the enemy to an ambush point. Keep your eyes open for signs that tell you someone may be in trouble. When you ask someone how they are doing, don't just take the first response, as it sometimes is just a reflex answer. Ask again, "How are you really doing?"

When someone does invite your help, *thank them*. Their trust in you is a sign of respect that you should not take lightly. When they bare their heart, handle it with the utmost care. Do all you can to remain worthy of their trust. Don't break that trust by sharing information with anyone else unless you have permission or the situation is extreme and dangerous.

Listening is both a way to sustain trust *and* an important way to help someone who is under spiritual attack. Listen well, and don't jump in too quickly with fixes for their problems. The first thing most hurting people need is to know they're being heard and understood—that's your priority and goal. Once you've assured them—through open ears, by withholding "advice," and by nonthreatening questions—that they're not alone, then they will come to a point of readiness for your counsel.

As Dr. Curt Thompson affirms, when you listen to someone with genuine interest and compassion, you make it safe for them to risk "being known."[1] And that is a vital part of each believer's health as an individual, in relationship with God, and as an integrated, functioning part of Christ's body. By listening, you act as healer, drawing the other person into true security and significance in Christ.

2. As you read **2 Corinthians 10:3–5**; **Colossians 4:12**; and **Ephesians 6:10–18**, picture obeying these *together* in the context of your church family. Describe your duties as a soldier, helping when your brothers and sisters call.

_____

_____

_____

_____

_____

Sometimes "intruding" is an act of love. The following are good guidelines when approaching someone, particularly if they have not asked for help:

- Preserve their dignity. Try to minimize embarrassment by minimizing the number of people who have to know about the problem. Shelter the feeble flame of your friend's courage to do what's right while it strengthens and grows into resolve (**Gal. 6:1.**)

- Remember your desire is to help, not to judge. Before you approach them about their fault, you should first examine your motives as well as deal with that same fault if it lies in you. Then you will be better prepared to help the other person (**Matt. 7:1–5**).

- Be honest and gracious. Be neither blunt nor evasive, but prayerfully prepare to speak the truth in love (**Eph. 4:15**).

1. Curt Thompson, "Anatomy of the Soul," *Being Known*, http://www.beingknown.com/anatomy-of-the-soul/.

Though we live in the world, we do not wage war as the world does. The weapons we fight with are not the weapons of the world. On the contrary, they have divine power to demolish strongholds. We demolish arguments and every pretension that sets itself up against the knowledge of God, and we take captive every thought to make it obedient to Christ. (2 Cor. 10:3–5)

Epaphras . . . is always wrestling in prayer for you, that you may stand firm in all the will of God, mature and fully assured. (Col. 4:12)

Finally, be strong in the Lord and in his mighty power. Put on the full armor of God so that you can take your stand against the devil's schemes. For our struggle is not against flesh and blood, but against the rulers, against the authorities, against the powers of this dark world and against the spiritual forces of evil in the heavenly realms. Therefore put on the full armor of God, so that when the day of evil comes, you may be able to stand your ground, and after you have done everything, to stand. Stand firm then, with the belt of truth buckled around your waist, with the breastplate of righteousness in place, and with your feet fitted with the readiness that comes from the gospel of peace. In addition to all this, take up the shield of faith, with which you can extinguish all the flaming arrows of the evil one. Take the helmet of salvation and the sword of the Spirit, which is the word of God.

And pray in the Spirit on all occasions with all kinds of prayers and requests. With this in mind, be alert and always keep on praying for all the Lord's people. (Eph. 6:10–18)

Brothers and sisters, if someone is caught in a sin, you who live by the Spirit should restore that person gently. But watch yourselves, or you also may be tempted. (Gal. 6:1)

Judge not, that you be not judged. For with the judgment you pronounce you will be judged, and with the measure you use it will be measured to you. Why do you see the speck that is in your brother's eye, but do not notice the log that is in your own eye? Or how can you say to your brother, "Let me take the speck out of your eye," when there is the log in your own eye? You hypocrite, first take the log out of your own eye, and then you will see clearly to take the speck out of your brother's eye. (Matt 7:1–5 ESV)

Speaking the truth in love, we will grow to become in every respect the mature body of him who is the head, that is, Christ. (Eph. 4:15)

My dear brothers and sisters, take note of this: Everyone should be quick to listen, slow to speak and slow to become angry. (James 1:19)

- Explain, then listen (**James 1:19**). Share briefly the reasons for your concern. Then genuinely listen to your friend's response, hopefully either confirming or alleviating your concern.

If the issue is serious and may present danger—spiritually, mentally, or physically—to the person or those around him or her, you may need to confront ongoing resistance with bluntness and intervention. But bathe your efforts continuously in prayer, and seek wisdom from one or two mature believers. This is not gossip if you are sharing something with those who can help. Your motive is to help, and every action you take is to restore, not to hurt.

3. What are a few ways you might recognize a brother's or sister's need for help—through words or behavior patterns—even if they don't ask?

   _____

   _____

   _____

4. What are some ways you might talk yourself out of helping a fellow soldier?

   _____

   _____

   _____

   _____

5. Have you ever tried to help a fellow believer and it didn't go well? Or has someone else interfered in your life in an unwelcome way? If so, describe what happened. How can you learn from such experiences and remain open to stepping into another person's life when necessary?

   _____

   _____

   _____

Day 4: Accountability

The word *accountability* has been subtly stolen from us by our enemy. He's happy to distort accountability by either of two errors.

Many call their small groups "accountability groups," but all they do is share their struggles. They don't do anything to help one another change, usually because they don't know how and they don't want to risk losing the relationship by interjecting difficult truth. These people would say they're acting in the interest of "relationship" and "grace" toward each other. But without the courage it takes to be honest and even challenge, change is just a nice idea. Without the willingness to allow others to speak into your life, you don't experience what life-changing relationship can be.

Or, from a different angle, many "accountability" partners genuinely want to put the emphasis on "truth," but they do so at the expense of grace and relationship—usually because they've never learned the importance of love as the necessary motive and method for everything we do. In our God's universe we live falsely when we speak without love.

1. Have you ever had an experience when accountability worked or didn't work for you? If so, describe what happened and why it did or didn't work.

   _____

   _____

   _____

Real discipleship requires the disciple-maker's ownership of his authority—and the disciple's recognition of that authority—to lead the new disciple to biblical answers, to life change. Equally important is the understanding that we are called to submit to our leaders (**Heb. 13:17**) and to one another (**Eph. 5:21**). Even if we are not being discipled by another, we still understand that

Have confidence in your leaders and submit to their authority, because they keep watch over you as those who must give an account. (Heb. 13:17)

Submit to one another out of reverence for Christ. (Eph. 5:21)

humility is a part of spiritual maturity. When a person challenges us, we can either become defensive or we can seek to discover if God is trying to speak to us through that brother or sister. We test their words by the Word of God, and we know God uses people in our lives.

Real accountability requires honest sharing from a disciple with the disciple-maker and then going to Scripture for right beliefs, as well as right actions and attitudes, guided by the Lord's Word. It requires the disciple both to desire change and to receive feedback and support as part of the process. But there is more to it than that. Real accountability has teeth to it. It has power because we give it power—we allow people to ask us hard questions and expect change from us. This is especially true when it comes from the authority God has instituted in the church, home, or world, but again, even friends must be allowed to hold us accountable when they speak God's truth to us. The one who seeks accountability is willing to submit, and the other must be willing to speak truth in love (**Prov. 27:17**).

A man recently told me he was struggling with porn and wanted help. He was brokenhearted, and I felt he really wanted to change. So I asked, "Are you willing to trust me and do what I ask you to do?"

He paused and said, "I have tried to quit for years, and nothing I have tried has worked. So, yes."

I recognized true repentance in him, not just worldly sorrow (2 Cor. 7:10), because he didn't qualify his answer. He truly was willing to do anything. So we made a plan together. I helped him find and install filters on his phone and computer. I helped him plan to tell his wife about his struggle and to share what he and I were going to do about it. I started receiving weekly reports from his computer filtering program about how he was doing. I got permission from him to discuss his struggle with his wife as well, because I wanted to know for sure that he had shared it with her and she understood the depth of the problem and his desire to beat it. He joined a sexual purity group in our church, and he recruited his closest Christian friend for prayer. I've been checking

Iron sharpens iron,
and one man [or woman] sharpens
another. (Prov. 27:17 ESV)

in with him after our men's group and texting him weekly, and I also check in with his wife to see how she thinks he's doing.

There's more to our plan, and he has submitted to every detail—not because I am his pastor and he has to, but because he is willing to submit to another person who will help him conquer his sin.

This is only one of many possible recipes for healthy accountability. While some basic components seem to apply for everyone, I adapt the formula to each individual I help.

2. From the example you just read, what are a few components that might be wise to include in any accountability plan? Why do these seem universal and nonnegotiable?

_____

_____

_____

3. Are there any other components you would add in all or some cases? If so, what are they?

_____

_____

_____

A woman recently told me she was mad at me. I was shocked, because her husband has been in my small group for years, and I have tried hard to help her by discipling her husband. She told me that my group wasn't really a discipleship group, because there was no accountability. I was surprised and asked what she meant. She shared that she had been struggling with her husband for the last year, and no one was holding him accountable for his failings.

I explained that every week in our small group I share my struggles. And likewise I go around the group and ask each man to share what is happening in his life. We then spend time listening to God's Word (through study and discussion) and creating plans of action for individual life change. Every week I ask her husband whether he is struggling with anything, and he consistently says no or shares about something other than his marriage.

"I can't read his mind," I said. "This is the first time either of you has shared any marriage difficulties with me."

No accountability relationship will work without honesty. Someone has to blow the trumpet.

4. Name some people you could blow the trumpet to when you are struggling.

_____

_____

_____

5. If you can't think of anyone for question 4, what are some steps you could take to start to build that kind of relationship?

_____

_____

_____

6. Authentic, mutual accountability in relationship is a necessary step toward any Jesus-follower's spiritual growth. Consider the following suggestions for two-way accountability commitments, and write down any thoughts about these to discuss with your group.

   • I accept that I need accountability from others. God uses spiritual authority in the human realm as a tool to help people grow. It's called discipleship, and it's essential to functioning well as part of the spiritual family.

   • I will be honest and allow others to ask how I'm progressing on my pathway toward spiritual maturity.

   • I will be honest if I fail and will allow others to pick me back up.

   • I will consistently follow through when others ask for help.

   • I will consistently ask the hard questions that others want me to ask. These hard questions include, for example, "How are you really doing in your marriage? In your time alone with God? With your kids?"

   _____

   _____

   _____

Day 5: Wounds of a Friend

The word *friendship* has also been stolen and so has lost its meaning among many Jesus-followers. We live in a culture where one of the rules is, you never rat out a friend. You back a friend's play no matter what, even if he or she is wrong. Yes, Scripture tells us that loyalty is important and that love means laying down your life for a friend, but God's version of friendship requires that you love so much that you give what the person needs, even when they don't like it. A true friend is willing, not just to risk life, but even to risk losing the other person's love in order to save them.

I was once confronted by a guy. It wasn't tactful, and I didn't immediately think he was right, but I have a policy about receiving confrontation as a potential gift. So in response I smiled at the man and said, "Thank you for being courageous enough to tell me the truth about how you see things. I respect you already just for saying it *to* me and not *about* me to others. I will pray about it and get some wise counsel to confirm what you have said. I'm not sure I agree with you, but I respect you. Thank you."

After following through on what I said I would do, I called and asked him to meet with me, and we discussed his criticism and my response.

I believe the best way to cut off the enemy from dividing us is to do our best to create a culture where honesty is honored. It's wise to allow people to speak into our lives rather than bury issues that might be valid. Among other benefits, our openness might allow an opportunity for resolution of some offense we're not even aware of; remaining closed might allow the devil to gain a foothold of bitterness in the other person's life. And, of course, it's in our own best interest to discover legitimate ways we can grow in becoming more like Christ.

Our Father often speaks to us through our brothers and sisters. So one way we can yield to Him in faith and love is to keep an open door for the potential "wounds" of others. Be careful not to scare away people who might be the Lord's messengers.

1. How would you describe yourself?
   - ☐ I'm closed to all criticism, and people know it.
   - ☐ I act like I'm listening, but inside I'm ignoring them or forming an answer to rebut their perspective.
   - ☐ My antenna's up, but I act like I'm not listening.
   - ☐ I listen, I consider, I pray, and then I do whatever seems right.
   - ☐ I'm everyone's punching bag, and I resent it, but no one knows I feel that way.
   - ☐ I believe everything anyone says about me.
   - ☐ Other:

2. What is one step you could take toward a healthy "open-door policy"?

   _____

   _____

   _____

A true friend is willing to wound you by telling you the truth because they want what is best for you. They will risk losing your friendship, as painful as that could be, if they know you are on a path to destruction. They not only call you out, they *call you up*.

One of my fellow staff members recently told me how grateful he was for a friend who had "called him up." I first thought he meant the friend had called him on the phone, but as he told the story I realized he had a different meaning. In a unique way, he was saying that, by confronting him, the friend had called him *up—upward* to higher ground, toward greater holiness and Christlikeness. His friend had said, "I know you love Jesus, and I want to share with you that I love you. But right now you are not behaving consistently with who you really are." In other words, "You are so much more than your current decisions and behaviors."

What a loving thing to do for a friend, to provide a reminder of what they really want most, to prod them upward toward who you know they really want to be. To say hard things in a way that shows our hearts for them. When we multiply kisses (tell people only what they want to hear), God says we are showing *ourselves* to be the enemy (**Prov. 27:6**).

It's important that you act and speak with grace and obvious love, in a way that does not press the other person's flesh buttons. Some people have confronted me (and they were right), but the way they did it made it hard for me to hear. I had to weed through the natural responses of my flesh to get to the truth.

Share the right things with the right heart. Pain is inevitable, but a wound inflicted for love can rescue someone from disaster. It is the upward call to a higher standard.

Wounds from a friend can be trusted,
but an enemy multiplies kisses.
(Prov. 27:6)

3. Describe a time when you or someone you know inflicted a loving wound and saw good come out of it. Why did it work?

   ---

4. How would you like to be confronted? What signals would send you the message that you are loved even while you are hearing something difficult?

   ---

5. Have you been wounded by criticism? If so, what would help you get through that experience so that it doesn't contaminate your relationships with friends who really do want what is best for you?

   ---

6. What are the key insights you have had in Week 9 of this study? What do you want to take from this week and apply to your life?

   ---

7. What are the main things you have learned from this study of *The Power of Together*? Look back through this workbook and write down at least three things that you want to take with you into your life. Share them with your group.

_____

_____

_____

Growing Together

An optional Week 10 review and celebration is listed on the next page.

Day 1: In your group it would be a good idea to go through each lie and temptation in questions 3 and 4 to ensure everyone knows what the biblical truth is for each one. Review your answer to questions 6 and 7 and discuss them with the group.

Day 2: Share some examples from question 8 where the group has helped its members with struggles or issues.

Day 3: Review the guidelines for "intruding" listed before question 3. Discuss how "intruding" can be an act of love.

Day 4: Together with your group, adjust and adapt the accountability list in question 6 so that it serves your relationships best. Once your group has agreed on the form of its commitments, encourage each person to voice these commitments to at least one other member sometime during the next seven days—now or later, in person, by phone or Skype, by email or text.

Remember this: When doing battle with the enemy and with your sinful nature, you need the Spirit of God, the Word of God, and the people of God to help you on the mission of God.

Day 5: Discuss question 4. Then have each group member share at least one answer to question 7.

With your group, celebrate your completion of this workbook process. Have some special refreshments to make your final meeting partly a party. Talk about what you've gained from the group, and pray a blessing over each member. If you've committed to becoming accountable to one another or to the group leader, talk about how that will be played out as you go forward. What will your group do next?

Optional Week 10 Review & Celebration

If you have time, you can plan a tenth meeting for review and celebration. This will allow you to take time to pray over each group member in greater depth. For each person, allow other members to thank God for what that person has contributed to your group. Acknowledge the gifts this person has exercised. Ask God to work in this person's life to bring him or her to maturity. Pray for the person's needs. Spend at least five minutes soaking each person in prayer before moving on to the next person.

Hopefully, this is not the end for your group but the beginning of a deepening set of relationships that will draw each member to maturity in Christ.

We always thank God for all of you and continually mention you in our prayers. We remember before our God and Father your work produced by faith, your labor prompted by love, and your endurance inspired by hope in our Lord Jesus Christ. (1 Thess. 1:2–3)

I thank my God every time I remember you. In all my prayers for all of you, I always pray with joy because of your partnership in the gospel from the first day until now, being confident of this, that he who began a good work in you will carry it on to completion until the day of Christ Jesus. (Phil. 1:3–6)

For Group Leaders

The goal of your small group is to help its members grow in their ability to love others well. The content and questions aim not just at learning information but at putting it into practice. Your group is a place for members to practice relationships of love.

Therefore, if you meet for ninety minutes, consider structuring your meeting like this:

15 minutes   Warm-up question

55 minutes   Group discussion

20 minutes   Prayer for one another

Following are suggested warm-up questions for each week. Give everyone a chance to respond. As the leader, you usually won't answer the discussion questions yourself, but you should participate in answering the warm-up question.

Before each meeting, go through the week's questions, review the Growing Together section at the end of each week, and choose any additional questions you think will be most helpful for group discussion. Hopefully group members will have written their answers to the questions, but usually much more can be said. Aim at having them interact with one another rather than just reading their answers to the questions.

At the end of your meeting, ask, "How can we pray for you?" If your group contains ten or more people, consider dividing into groups of five or six people for prayer. This will give everyone a chance to pray aloud for others if they wish to do so. No one should be obliged to pray aloud. Aim for making it normal for members to ask for prayer—not a sign of weakness. You can set an example by telling the group how they can pray for you.

Note that you have an option to add a Week 10 review and celebration that gives the group more time for wrap-up, prayer, and future plans.

Week 1 Warm-up Question

- In the process of coming to faith in Jesus, some of us have one big turning point, while others have a series of smaller turning points. What was one turning point for you? How old were you?

Week 2 Warm-up Question

- What role did relationships play in your conversion to following Jesus? If they played no role, you can say so.

Week 3 Warm-up Question

- Think of someone who has been a good friend to you. What has that person done that marks him or her as a good friend?

Week 4 Warm-up Question

- Describe a positive encounter you have had with a brother or sister at church. This could be your current church or a former church. Don't name names.

Week 5 Warm-up Question

- Describe a positive experience you have had with someone in authority over you, whether as a child or an adult. This could be with a parent, a teacher, a coach, a boss, a government official, a pastor, or any other authority figure.

Week 6 Warm-up Question

- When you were growing up, how did your parents/caregivers deal with disagreements?

Week 7 Warm-up Question

- When, if ever, have you experienced the benefits of teamwork?

Week 8 Warm-up Question

- When have you experienced a rough time in your life when you needed other people's help and support? (If the answer is "never," it's okay to say so.)

Week 9 Warm-up Question

- What is one way you have experienced the spiritual battle, either currently or in the past?

Optional Week 10 Review & Celebration

Jim Putman is the founder and senior pastor of Real Life Ministries in Post Falls, Idaho.

Real Life Ministries began as a small group in 1998 and has grown to a membership of more than eight thousand people. The church was launched with a commitment to discipleship and the model of discipleship Jesus practiced, which is called "Relational Discipleship." Ninety percent of the people are active in small groups. *Outreach Magazine* continually lists Real Life Ministries among the top one hundred most influential churches in America.

Jim is also the founding leader of the new Relational Discipleship Network. Jim holds degrees from Boise State University and Boise Bible College. Each year his teaching ministry reaches hundreds of thousands across the nation through speaking conferences, the web, radio, and weekend services.

He is the author of four books: *The Power of Together*, the companion to this workbook; *Church Is a Team Sport*; and *Real Life Discipleship* and *Real Life Discipleship Workbook* (with Avery Willis and others).

Jim's passion is discipleship through small groups. With his background in sports and coaching, he believes in the value of strong coaching as a means to disciple others.

He lives with his wife and three sons in scenic northern Idaho.

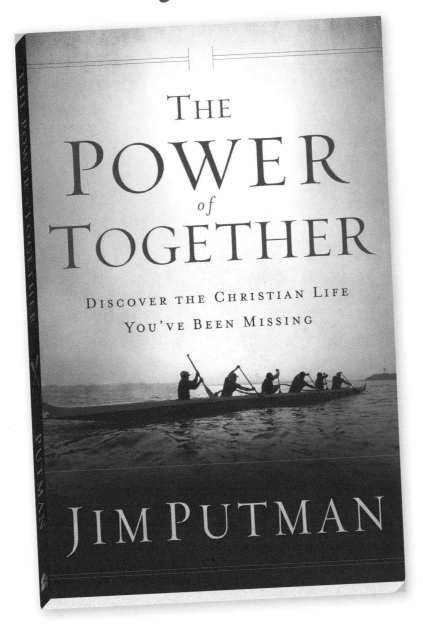

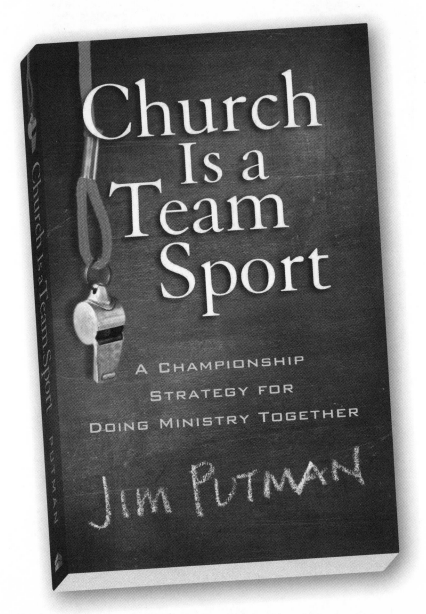